AGENCY
ETHICS
FAIR HOUSING LAWS
TRUST FUND HANDLING
CALIFORNIA RISK MANAGEMENT

KAPLAN PROFESSIONAL SCHOOLS

This publication is designed to provide accurate and authoritative information in regard to the subject matter covered. It is sold with the understanding that the publisher is not engaged in rendering legal, accounting, or other professional service. If legal advice or other expert assistance is required, the services of a competent professional should be sought.

President: Roy Lipner
Vice President, General Manager: Mehul Patel
Vice President of Product Development & Publishing: Evan M. Butterfield
Managing Editor: Kate DeVivo
Senior Development Editor: Tony Peregrin
Director of Production: Daniel Frey
Production Editor: Samantha Raue
Creative Director: Lucy Jenkins

Published by Dearborn™ Real Estate Education

    30 South Wacker Drive
    Chicago, Illinois 60606-7481
    (312) 836-4400
    www.dearbornRE.com

Printed in the United States of America

07 08 09 10 9 8 7 6 5 4 3 2 1

COURSE 1: AGENCY

Unit 3   Loan Transactions: Unlawful Conduct   62

Unit 4   Suggestions for Professional Conduct   69

COURSE 3: FAIR HOUSING LAWS

COURSE 4: TRUST FUND HANDLING

COURSE 5: CALIFORNIA RISK MANAGEMENT

Unit 1

Introduction to Risk Management   171

Unit 2

Fraud, Misrepresentation, and Puffing   177

Unit 3

Risks Associated with Conflicts of Interest   181

Unit 4   **Risks Associated with Offers, Contracts, and Trust Funds   188**

Unit 5   **Risks Associated with Property Condition and Disclosures   192**

Unit 6   **Risks Associated with Employment, Antitrust, Fair Housing, and Advertising   199**

Unit 7   **Legal Responsibility   204**

Course 1: Agency

Introduction to Agency

The laws of agency govern the relationships between the broker, the salesperson, the buyer, and the seller in a real estate transaction. In the agency relationship, the agent and the principal agree that the agent is to act for the benefit of the principal.

The agent has the power to affect the legal relations of the principal. The agent must be faithful to the principal and use reasonable skill in the performance of duties. This duty is known as a fiduciary obligation. When an error, negligence, fraud, or possibly some other failure results in losses, the principal, as well as the agent, may be deemed responsible. It then becomes necessary to examine the duties, rights, and liabilities of the parties involved.

■ Statutory Basis of Agency

With regard to real estate transactions, there are four laws that apply to agency relationships in California:

1. Law of agency
2. Real estate law
3. Statute of frauds
4. Agency disclosure law

Law of Agency

The law of agency (Civil Code §2295) defines agency and identifies the ways in which the various types of agency can be created. It also describes the duties and liabilities of the parties (the principal and the agent) in their relationship with each other, and describes their duties and liabilities to third parties. This law applies to all agency relationships, not only to those in real estate. Dual agency is permissible only with the knowledge and consent of all parties in the transactions and is called disclosed dual agency.

Real Estate Law

Business and Professions Code §10176(d) provides that the real estate commissioner may suspend or revoke the real estate license of a person who has been guilty of "acting for more than one party in a transaction without the knowledge

3

or consent of all parties thereto." Such action is considered an "undisclosed dual agency." The person who acts in such a capacity is an undisclosed "dual agent."

Statute of Frauds

The statute of frauds, Civil Code §1624, requires that certain contracts *must be in writing* to be enforceable, including "an agreement authorizing or employing an agent . . . to purchase or sell real estate, or to lease real estate for a longer period than one year. . . ." Thus, a broker might be unable to enforce payment of a commission if his or her listing is not in writing and signed by the principal.

Agency Disclosure Law

The agency disclosure law for residential real estate transactions, Civil Code §2079 et seq., requires a licensee dealing in residential property (1) to provide a disclosure form to both buyer and seller explaining agency and (2) to confirm the agency relationship(s) of the licensee in the contract to purchase and sell the real property.

■ Unit 1 Review Quiz

1. The laws of agency apply exclusively to real estate licensees.
   a. True
   b. False

Principal-Agent Relationship

The California Civil Code §2295 defines an agent as "one who represents another, called the principal, in dealings with third persons. Such representation is called an agency." In real estate, a broker may be the agent of a seller, buyer, lender, borrower, landlord, or tenant.

The agent's actions within the scope of the agency relationship are deemed to be the actions of the principal, whether such actions are intentional, negligent, or innocent. Any knowledge possessed or notice received by the agent is imputed notice to the principal and vice versa. In other words, what one knows, the other knows.

■ Types of Agency

General vs. Special

Example

An infirm person might hire a general agent to handle *all transactions,* such as to sell a parcel of real estate, to sign for personal services contracts, and to complete investment transactions. This general agent, acting on behalf of the principal, might then hire a special agent—a real estate licensee—to assist in the real estate sales transaction.

Real estate brokers are normally special agents, employed for the specific purpose of procuring a buyer or seller or tenant for a parcel of real property. Real estate salespersons are also special agents who assist the broker in duties as an agent of the broker.

Power of attorney. A power of attorney is a written instrument by which a principal appoints an attorney-in-fact as agent and confers upon the agent the authority to act on behalf of the principal. The authority may be general, to transact all business, or special, to transact limited business.

Single vs. Dual and Divided Agency

In a single agency, an agent represents only one principal party. In a dual agency, an agent represents both principal parties, such as the seller and the buyer. This arrangement requires the knowledge and consent of all parties.

Acting as a representative for both parties in a transaction without their knowledge or consent is divided agency and is both a breach of fiduciary duty as well as a violation of the law. Such a violation may subject a real estate licensee to disciplinary action.

Gratuitous agency. Compensation is not required to establish an agency relationship. An agency that does not involve compensation is called a gratuitous agency.

Example

A licensee might agree to find a parcel of land for a retail developer without an arrangement to be compensated by the developer. The agent might undertake this kind of agency with the expectation of future leasing commissions.

■ Creation of Agency

An agency relationship is created when the principal authorizes or is deemed to authorize the agent to act on his or her behalf in transactions with others. The agency can be created in any of three ways:

1. By agreement between the parties, express or implied, sometimes referred to as "actual agency"
2. By the principal's ratification of an agent's previously unauthorized act, also a form of "actual agency"
3. "Ostensible agency" by "estoppel"

Express or Implied Agreement

An agency relationship does not depend on the existence of a written contract. A broker who acts with no written listing agreement may still be subject to all the fiduciary obligations imposed by the principal-agent relationship.

Although no formal contract is required to create an agency relationship, there must be an intention by the parties, either express or implied, to create such a relationship. This intent may be manifested by the parties' words or conduct or by the surrounding facts and circumstances.

Example

A potential seller, although unwilling to negotiate a listing agreement, may nevertheless authorize a licensee to solicit purchase offers and furnish the licensee with information concerning the property. This authorization would constitute an express agreement.

In making representations concerning the property and soliciting offers, the licensee would be acting as the seller's agent. The seller could be liable for any torts the licensee might commit in connection with these activities. Meanwhile, the licensee owes fiduciary duties to the seller just as if a written contract existed.

If the broker assists the buyer of the seller's property in obtaining financing after the purchase contract has been negotiated, the broker may also have become the buyer's agent, at least for purposes relating to financing, under an implied agreement.

Ratification

An agency may also be created by the principal's acceptance, or ratification, of a previously unauthorized action by another individual. Ratification normally results when the purported agent has held himself or herself out as representing the principal, and the principal then accepts the benefits of the purported agent's actions.

Example

A certain real estate licensee is purporting to act as an owner's agent to sell land. The agent accepts a portion of the purchase price from a prospective purchaser. The owner subsequently conveys the land to the purchaser and notifies the licensee in writing not to return the money received. In this case, a court would likely hold that the owner's actions constituted ratification of the licensee's status as an agent.

Estoppel, or Ostensible Agency

Agency by estoppel, or ostensible agency, results when the principal, either intentionally or negligently, causes a third party to believe that another person is the principal's agent, and the third party relies on that belief. The principal's statements, actions, or inaction lead the third party to believe that the person is acting as an agent. When this happens, the principal will be "estopped"—prohibited or barred—from later asserting that the agent was not acting on the principal's behalf.

Example

A seller advertised a property for sale through a particular realty firm. The broker who received the deposit in response to the ad was not a member of that firm, but did occupy office space in the firm's offices. When the broker disappeared with the money, the court allowed the prospective purchaser to recover her lost money from the realty firm on the theory that the firm had allowed the plaintiff to believe the absconding broker was its agent.

Judicial Interpretation

California courts may impute an agency relationship and fiduciary obligations to a licensee when they perceive a need to protect the interests of a buyer or seller.

"Whenever the acts or omissions of a licensee cause injury in a real estate transaction, there is a compelling reason to find him an agent. . . . No California decision has held a licensee exempt from fiduciary obligations to the seller when the licensee has in fact acted to the seller's detriment." (*Skopp v. Weaver*, 16 Cal. 3d 432)

Example

A certain buyer's broker accepts a deposit on a property from his buyers and deposits it in his trust account over the weekend. The seller, informed of the offer, turns down a full-price offer from another buyer. On Monday morning, the broker's buyers back out, and the broker returns their deposit. The seller, having lost a buyer as well as her deposit, sues the buyer's broker for the deposit. The court supports the claim, asserting the broker was acting on behalf of the seller in tendering (and mishandling!) the deposit.

Commission

A licensee's ability to enforce payment of a commission without a written agreement is an issue not based on general principles of agency, but rather on the statute of frauds. Under the California statute of frauds (Civil Code §1624), "an agreement authorizing or employing an agent, broker, or other person to purchase or sell real estate, or to lease real estate for a longer period than one year" must be in writing and signed by the party to be charged or his or her agent.

■ Termination of Agency

An agency may be terminated by the following:

- Agreement of the parties
- Expiration of its term (e.g., termination date of listing)
- Extinction of its subject (the work was completed or the subject matter is destroyed)
- Death or incapacity of either the agent or the principal
- Renunciation by the agent (e.g., the agent quits)
- Revocation by the principal (e.g., the principal cancels the listing)

Expiration

The listing agreement terminates after the date specified in the listing agreement, which is often 90 days. In this case, the listing agreement would terminate on the 91st day. However, the broker may be entitled to a commission after the termination date of a listing if the broker complies with the "safety clause" in the listing agreement.

Extinction

The destruction of the property automatically terminates a listing or management agency agreement in the absence of any agreement to the contrary. In other words, impossibility terminates the agency. For example, if an agent were employed to find a tenant for a property, the destruction of that property would terminate the agency.

Death

Listing agreements are personal services contracts between parties. Since one cannot come back from the dead, there is no way to enforce such agreements in the event the agent dies. Thus, a broker's death cancels all listings held by him or her. For this reason, many real estate companies elect the corporate form of ownership. The corporation holds the real estate broker's license and the agency relationships with clients, which can then survive the individual broker. Death of the principal also terminates the agency. (If the sales associate dies, it does not affect the relationship because you can hire another.)

Renunciation

Under certain circumstances, the agent has the right to terminate the agreement and this would be done through renunciation. This could occur if the principal were to ask the agent to perform a discriminatory act, which would be illegal. However, if a party wrongfully breaches the agency, that party could be liable for damages.

Incapacity of Agent or Principal

If the agent is no longer capable of acting as an agent or the principal becomes mentally incapacitated, the agency terminates. An agent who loses his or her license would be incapable of performance, so the agency would terminate.

Revocation

Although the principal usually has the *power* to revoke the agency, he or she may not have the *right* to do so. This means that a principal who revokes the agency without cause or reason may be held liable for breach of contract.

Example

A principal who revokes a listing may be liable for payment of the broker's commission or other unreimbursed expenses incurred on the principal's behalf. Nevertheless, the revocation terminates the agency.

■ Authority of the Agent

The agency relationship confers authority to the agent to do everything necessary and proper to achieve the object of the agency. The forms of authority are actual and ostensible.

Actual vs. Ostensible Authority

The agent's **actual authority** is that which the principal has intentionally conferred.

The agent's **ostensible authority** is the authority the principal causes a third party to believe the agent possesses (agency by estoppel).

Example

A principal hires an agent to find an apartment. The agent finds a property and places a deposit on it without the prior consent of the principal. When the principal finds out, she is delighted and says nothing to the landlord. In this case, the agent had the actual authority to locate a property and the ostensible authority to place deposits, since the principal, by her silence, led the landlord to believe such authority had been granted to the agent.

■ Liability of Principal

According to Civil Code §2330, the acts of the agent are the acts of the principal when the agent is acting within the scope of the agency. Therefore, the principal is liable for such acts of the agent. This liability extends to subagents and includes liability for negligence and misrepresentation. The principal bears the risk of loss of the buyer's deposit caused by the negligence or fraud of the agent.

If the agent suffers a personal loss because he or she followed the instructions of the principal, the principal will be obligated to the agent for that loss.

Notice to Either, Notice to Both

Both principal and agent are deemed to have notice of whatever either has notice of. Thus, if an agent has received notice of a material fact, it is assumed that the principal has likewise been notified. The implication is that principals and agents should, in the exercise of ordinary care and diligence, communicate with one another.

Example

An inspector informs the seller's agent that the seller's property has a serious septic problem. If the agent continues to market the home without disclosing the defect, the seller is liable for misrepresentation, whether the agent informs the seller of the defect or not. The legal assumption is that both parties received the inspector's notice.

Torts of the Agent

Agents are personally liable for their torts and crimes even when committed at the direction of the principal. A tort is a civil wrong or violation of a duty. Civil wrongs that are torts include libel, slander, trespass, assault, negligent injury to others, etc. Some torts such as assault or trespass can also be crimes.

A principal is responsible to third persons for negligence of the agent in the transaction of the business of the agency, including wrongful acts committed by the agent in transaction of such business, and for the agent's willful omission to fulfill the obligations of the principal (Civil Code §2338).

Example

Suppose that the principal in the previous example had disclosed the defect in the septic system to the agent, and that the agent had willfully continued to represent the property as having no known problem with the septic system. If damages result, the principal is liable to the buyers for failure to disclose a material defect.

■ Delegation of Duties to Other Agents

A person to whom an agent delegates agency powers is a *subagent*. Historically, subagency in real estate was created through the multiple listing service rules.

Brokers, however, may delegate duties for which a real estate license is required only to other brokers and to sales licensees employed by the broker. This delegation to salespersons does not constitute subagency. Rather, the licensee becomes an agent of the broker. Duties requiring a license are specifically listed in Business and Professions Code §10131.

Example

A broker obtains an exclusive listing on a new subdivision development complete with model homes. To handle the flow of prospective buyers, the broker stations his unlicensed sales assistant in one of the models. The assistant is supposed to "take names." However, the broker encourages the assistant to point out the unique benefits of the subdivision to all prospects. The broker has committed an illegal delegation of duties by asking an unlicensed person to perform acts for which a licence is required.

■ Employee vs. Independent Contractor

Agents in an agency relationship may be employed as employees or as independent contractors, depending on issues of control, liability, and law.

Employee

An **employee** is subjected to the control of the **employer** as to the results of the individual's work, as well as how the results are to be achieved. An employee *may or may not be authorized to act as an agent*. This is determined by whether the employee has been authorized to act on behalf of the **principal** with third parties. This can also apply to independent contractors who can also be authorized to act on behalf of a principal with third parties.

Example

If a broker supervises and controls the time, place, and methods of work of her secretary, the secretary is an employee.

Independent Contractor

If the **employer** does not exercise control over how the worker is to accomplish a particular task, the worker would probably be an **independent contractor**.

Example

An owner engages a general contractor to build a house. The owner does not tell the contractor how to accomplish the construction. He hires the contractor to build in accordance with plans and specifications in the manner the contractor deems proper. The builder would clearly quality as an independent contractor.

Respondent Superior

A major distinction between an employee versus an independent contractor relationship is the employer's liability for the employee's acts. Under the principle of *respondent superior*, the employer is liable for acts the employee commits in the course and scope of performance of the services for which the employee was engaged. In contrast, the employer is not liable for an independent contractor's acts unless the independent contractor is also an agent of the employer.

Broker and salesperson.   The relationship between a broker and salesperson contains elements of both employer and employee and employer and independent contractor. The broker is liable for the acts of his or her salespeople, hence the element of employer-employee. On the other hand, salespeople are compensated based on their results, not their time spent on the job. For this reason, the tax code allows a salesperson to be treated as an independent contractor, while the Business and Professions Code considers a salesperson to be an employee. An independent contractor agreement will not allow the broker to escape liability for the acts and omissions of salespersons. Under the real estate law, a licensed salesperson could be in either an employee-employer or an independent contractor relationship with a broker but will always be an employee in the eyes of the Department of Real Estate.

Independent Contractor Agreement

It is common in the real estate industry to identify a salesperson as an independent contractor in a written contract between broker and salesperson. Such a contractual designation, however, is not absolute. For some purposes, a salesperson is considered the broker's employee, regardless of the formal characterization of the relationship.

Liability for salesperson's actions.   The broker is required by law to exercise reasonable supervision over salesperson. This requirement, under the real estate law and for purposes of civil liability, makes a salesperson under a broker an employee and not an independent contractor.

Taxes

Taxing authorities, such as the Internal Revenue Service, may accept the designation of a worker as an independent contractor from the standpoint of both broker and salesperson, regardless of how real estate law treats the relationship.

■ Unit 2 Review Quiz

1. Ona, wishing to sell her house, grants her brother a general power of attorney. The brother

   a. may not transact other business on behalf of his sister.

   b. could represent the buyer if he had a license.

   c. has insufficient authority to complete the task.

   d. has full authority to seek buyers for the property.

2. An agent knew that a property would be coming on the market, since the homeowner had told the agent about an upcoming job transfer. When the agent produced a full-price buyer for the property, a completely surprised seller informed the agent that he would consider the offer, but was not liable for any commission, since there was no listing agreement. In this case,

   a. the seller could become liable for the commission if he accepts the offer that includes the commission.

   b. the seller owes the agent a commission for producing a ready, willing, and able buyer.

   c. the agent was correct in claiming a commission under an implied agency with the seller.

   d. the agent can sue for commission.

3. The agent in question 2 knew that a property would be coming on the market and, although there was no listing agreement, produced a bona fide buyer for the property. If the seller accepts this buyer's offer, the seller may be liable for paying the agent a commission.

   a. True

   b. False

4. A seller is thoroughly unsatisfied with an agent's performance and decides to list with another brokerage. The seller cancels the agreement and refuses to pay for the agent's advertising and promotional expenses. Since the agent performed unsatisfactorily, the agent's only recourse is to comply and absorb the marketing expenses.

   a. True

   b. False

5. An agent orders termite treatment on her principal's vacation home in order to remedy a positive finding by the pest control inspector. When the owner finds out, she notifies the inspector immediately that she will not pay the $700 bill. She had not given the agent the authority to order the treatment, although she had given the authority to perform routine maintenance tasks. The pest control inspector would be unable to collect on the bill from the owner, since the owner did not authorize the treatment.

   a. True

   b. False

6. A real estate licensee works full-time for a fast-food franchise. The agent maintains regular office hours at the company, and must follow the company's methods for analyzing potential restaurant sites. The licensee is paid a commission for every site she puts under lease. The person would most likely be considered an employee of the franchise.

   a. True

   b. False

3

Licensee's Duties to Principal in a Real Estate Transaction

Once an agency relationship has been established, the agent owes a number of fiduciary duties to the principal as established by general laws of agency. In addition, California real estate laws and the Department of Real Estate (DRE) impose additional duties specifically on real estate licensees, including disclosure, care, skill, diligence, and the duty to investigate.

■ General Fiduciary Duties

Agents owe principals the universal fiduciary duties of good faith, loyalty, diligence, and faithful service. General agency law imposes these duties in all agency relationships, not only those involving real property.

Diligence and Good Faith

All the agent's actions must be aimed at accomplishing for the principal the purpose for which the agent was employed. It is improper for an agent to act for his or her own benefit in an agency situation.

Example

An owner asks an agent to list the owner's house. After surveying recent sales in the area and inspecting the property, the agent determines that it will probably sell for $100,000. However, the agent personally wants a quick sale, and advises the principal to list the house for $90,000. It sells for that price on the first day. In this case, the agent has breached fiduciary duty and will be subject to liability, unless (1) the owner expressed an interest in a quick sale and (2) the agent explained all the facts, including that the house would probably sell for $100,000 even though it might take longer.

Accounting

An agent has a duty to account to the principal for all property received by the agent arising out of the employment. The agent must account for all funds received or disbursed on behalf of the principal.

Loyalty

An agent cannot, without permission, disclose to third parties any confidential facts about the principal or agency that would not be in the principal's best interests. This duty continues even after the agency has terminated. For example, a dual agent cannot disclose information received in confidence, such as that the seller will accept less or the buyer will pay more.

Not Competing

The agent may not compete with the principal for the agent's own account, or for another, in matters relating to the subject of the agency.

Example

An agent is prohibited from obtaining an underpriced listing and then personally purchasing the same property with the knowledge that the property is underpriced.

Similarly, the agent would be violating his or her duty to obtain the underpriced listing and have his or her rich uncle acquire the property for immediate resale. This illegal practice is known as "secret profit."

■ Duties under Real Estate Law

The California real estate law imposes additional duties on licensees while acting as agents in real estate transactions. Some are similar to the duties imposed by general agency law, while others are more stringent and apply only to real estate licensees. Violations of agency duties are grounds for license suspension or revocation.

Full Disclosure

The agent must disclose all material facts that might influence the principal with respect to the transaction or the principal's willingness to enter into it. A fact is deemed material if it would influence the principal's judgment or decision. Important disclosures, such as those defining the agency relationship, should be in writing. This gives licensees the protection of hard evidence of disclosure in case of a lawsuit.

Example

Consider an agent who knows before signing a listing agreement with a seller that a major department store is shopping for property in the area of the listed property. To the extent that the department store's interest will affect the listing price, the principal is entitled to know whatever facts the agent knows. The agent must disclose this fact to the principal.

Accounting

The agent has the duty at all times to account to the principal for all property received or held by the agent on the principal's behalf. The failure to account will subject the agent to disciplinary action, and any loss arising from such failure will subject the agent to civil liability to the principal.

Secret Profits

The agent may not make a **secret profit** in a transaction involving the subject matter of the agency. A secret profit is one that would be made by the agent separate from any commission but that results in one way or another from the transaction. If the agent plans to make a profit from the transaction, he or she must disclose this fact to the principal and obtain the principal's consent in order to retain the profit.

Example

An agent convinces her seller to accept a buyer's offer, knowing that the buyer is going to use a contractor who will give the agent a fee for referring the buyer's business. The agent must disclose this potential secret profit to the seller.

Disciplinary Action

Taking any secret profit subjects the licensee to disciplinary action by the DRE. In addition, the agent may be required to return the profit to the principal. This is true even if the transaction was otherwise fair to the principal and the principal received the full asking price.

■ Care, Skill, and Diligence

An agent is required to use "reasonable" care, skill, and diligence in the performance of all duties for the principal's benefit. "Reasonable" means the level of performance the law would expect of a "reasonable" real estate agent in similar circumstances. Negligence is interpreted as the breach of the duty to use that degree of care, skill, and diligence.

Standard of Care

If the agent has not met the standard expected of the "reasonable" licensee, he or she is negligent, has breached a duty to the principal, and may be held liable. Whether the agent's care, skill, and diligence were "reasonable" will ultimately be determined by the judge or jury in a civil action or by the real estate commissioner in a disciplinary action.

Skill and Diligence

When an agent is employed by the seller, he or she undertakes contractual duties set forth in the listing agreement. Most often, these are to use due diligence and skill to try to find a purchaser who is ready, willing, and able to purchase on the terms and conditions set forth in the listing agreement or other terms and conditions acceptable to the seller. Failure to perform these duties with skill and diligence may subject the agent to *liability* for breach of contract, as well as a breach of fiduciary duty.

Example

An agent lists a property, but then makes no effort to market it. The agent has breached the duty of diligence and may be subject to civil liability and DRE disciplinary action.

Licensee's Duty to Investigate

The licensee purports to be a knowledgeable practitioner in the real estate field, dealing with matters about which the general public is less skillful. Like any other expert, the licensee is required to know certain facts concerning the subject matter of the agency, or to investigate facts he or she may not know but is expected to know.

Increasing Expectations

Expanding case law and education requirements impose ever-greater duties of knowledge on the licensee. If a licensee does not know the answers to certain questions, the law requires that he or she inquire to discover them. Even if the questions never arise, the licensee may nevertheless have a duty to investigate certain matters concerning the property.

A good example of the expanding knowledge requirement is flood zone liability. Near rivers that are prone to flooding, the general danger of flooding needs to be disclosed. The specific 100-year flood zone disclosure under the new Natural Hazards Disclosure Statement may not be sufficient.

Level of Knowledge

The principal assumes that the licensee is an expert in real estate, familiar with aspects of real estate transactions about which the principal is less knowledgeable. If the licensee feels that his or her knowledge is inadequate in any given area, the licensee should so inform the principal before undertaking the agency relationship. At a minimum, the licensee is required either to know or to learn about any fact that would reasonably affect the principal's decision to sell or buy on the terms being negotiated.

Duty to Uncover Material Facts

A principal may not always disclosure all material facts concerning a transaction during the normal course of discussion about the property or the transaction. It is therefore incumbent on the licensee to interrogate the principal as to all material facts that might influence the principal's decision to buy or sell.

Example

A seller may not know about—or may not want buyers to know about—recent hearings underway to change a nearby residential zone to a commercial zone, a move that is widely considered to be adverse to local property values. Nevertheless, the agent could *not* be expected to know this development and must therefore ask the seller if there are any impending zoning changes that could impact the property's value.

■ Unit 3 Review Quiz

1. It is all right for an agent to act for his or her own benefit in an agency relationship as long as the principal shares in the agent's profits.

    a. True

    b. False

2. An agent has a listing agreement with a developer to sell homes in a new subdivision. He also enters into an agreement to represent some buyers in locating a home. He has informed both the developer and the buyers of his agency relationships, and they have consented to work with him. He shows the buyers a number of homes, starting with the homes in the new subdivision. When the buyers decline to make an offer on any of the subdivision homes, the agent proceeds to show them other homes. The broker has not violated his fiduciary duties.

    a. True

    b. False

3. A listing agent and the seller are trying to pin down the listing price. The seller asks the agent what a fair listing price would be, and the agent says that while a lot of the "beginners" in the brokerage community run CMAs to estimate value, he has all the confidence in the world that $209,000 is a good number, given current market conditions. They list at that price, and the property sells in no more than three days. The seller is delighted until the buyers inform her that they stole the property! Comparable properties, it turns out, are going for at least $225,000. At this point, the listing agent is exposed to liability for negligence.

    a. True

    b. False

4. A seller listed his newly renovated house with agent Bill. The renovations were a new family room and porch, which had just been completed the previous week. The seller put a reasonable price on the property, and it sold in two weeks because the market was red-hot. The buyers paid cash at closing and everyone was happy. The following week, the buyers were shocked to learn that a mechanic's lien had been placed on the property for billed work that had never been paid. Sure enough, the seller could not be found. In this case, it is most likely that

    a. agent Bill bears no liability since it would be a buyer's broker, not a seller's broker, who would be at fault for not knowing about the possibility of a mechanic's lien.

    b. agent Bill is negligent for failing to investigate whether the contractors had been paid for the renovation work.

    c. the mechanic's lien is invalid, since the property was sold to another owner.

    d. agent Bill has engaged in intentional fraud.

Duties to Third Parties

The agent's duty to parties other than the principal is the same as the principal's duty to other parties. These duties include honesty and fairness as well as the disclosure of material facts concerning the property. To the extent that the law requires the principal to disclose all material facts to the other party, the licensee must also disclose all material facts that are known or that should be known. In addition, licensees are prohibited from making secret profits.

■ Disclosure to the Buyer

The principle of **caveat emptor**—let the buyer beware—does not apply in real estate transactions. Recent legislative trends have emphasized seller accountability and consumer protection. In turn, listing agents must disclose to potential buyers all facts known or that should be known to the licensee that might be material to the buyer's purchase decision, regardless of how such disclosure might impact the outcome of the transaction.

Example

The swimming pool of a home has an underground leak that is not visible. In the past, this defect could have gone undisclosed to a buyer under the premise of caveat emptor: if there's a leak, it's the buyer's problem. Today, the leak has to be disclosed to avoid liability.

Know vs. Ought to Know

Traditionally, the licensee has been required to disclose all known material facts to third parties. The requirements did not extend to investigation or disclosure of facts that the licensee *ought to know*.

In 1984, the California Supreme Court upheld the decision in *Easton v. Strassburger*, which stated, in part, that "a broker is under a duty to disclose facts materially affecting the value or desirability of the property that are known to him or which through reasonable diligence *should be known to him*."

Inspection and Buyer Disclosure

Civil Code §§2079–2079.5 codified the principles established in *Easton v. Strassburger* requiring a real estate broker to "conduct a reasonably competent and diligent visual inspection of the property offered for sale" and disclose the facts that such an investigation would reveal.

■ Prohibition of Secret Profits

Both the courts and the Business and Professions Code have held that, because the real estate licensee has a special relationship with the public, he or she may not make a secret profit in a transaction with a third party.

Example

A broker falsely represented to a potential buyer that he had an exclusive listing on a property. After the buyer made an offer of $500 per acre, the broker secretly purchased the property for $400 per acre and resold it to the buyer at a profit of $100 per acre.

The Supreme Court, holding to the maxim that "no one should profit from his own wrong," required the broker to return the $100 per acre secret profit to the buyer.

■ Unit 4 Review Quiz

1. A listing agent in San Mateo County was trying to sell a property to an out-of-state buyer. Observing two cracks in the foundation, the buyer asked whether the cause was earthquakes, and, by the way, where the San Andreas Fault was located. The agent replied that the cracks were due to foundation settling, which was common. As to the fault, the agent "wasn't sure" where it was. Which of the following best characterizes the agent's situation concerning disclosure?

   a. He's in the clear.

   b. He's okay on the fault location, but in trouble on the foundation.

   c. He's okay on the foundation, but not okay on the fault location.

   d. He's risking trouble on both counts.

Whose Agent Are You?

Modern real estate brokerage is inherently confusing as to whom an agent "works for" as opposed to "works with." A buyer's or seller's misunderstanding of allegiances can easily lead to problems, conflicts, and monetary damages. It is therefore critical for an agent to identify which party to a transaction is his or her principal: the buyer, the seller, or both.

■ List Broker: Seller's Agent

A broker who has a written listing agreement with a seller is usually considered to be the seller's agent by virtue of the written contract (unless the listing agent elects to be a dual agent). No seller's agent may act as an agent for the buyer only when the selling agent is also the listing agent. (Civil Code §2079.18)

Possibility of Dual Agency

If the listing agent also procures the buyer, or is approached directly by the buyer, the broker may in some circumstances be deemed to be functioning as a dual agent, despite the fact that the seller is paying the broker's full commission. However, the fact that a broker acts as both the listing agent and the selling agent does not, of itself, create a dual agency.

■ Selling and Cooperating Brokers

Prior to 1988, because of MLS rules, a selling or cooperating licensee ran the risk of being considered a fiduciary of both seller and buyer. Prospective purchasers believed that the cooperating broker was working for the buyer's interests, when in fact the cooperating broker was typically a subagent, and therefore a fiduciary, of the seller. In theory, no one represented the buyer.

Subagency

When a listing was filed with an Association of REALTORS® multiple listing service, the listing agent extended an offer of subagency to all other members of that MLS. If a selling agent accepted the listing agent's offer of subagency, the selling agent became an agent of the seller and owed the seller the same fiduciary duties as the listing agent. However, a selling agent could reject the listing agent's offer of subagency and declare himself or herself an agent of the buyer exclusively.

Rejection of Subagency

Today, most of MLS's forms indicate whether or not the listing agent is making an offer of subagency. Even if an offer of subagency is extended, a selling agent can reject it and declare himself or herself the buyer's exclusive agent.

Judicial Rule

The courts consistently state that the existence of an agency relationship is a "question of fact"—meaning the answer will depend on the particular circumstances of a given case.

Example

In *Kruse v. Miller*, the sellers employed a broker, Garrity, to assist in the sale of their house. Garrity enlisted the cooperation of broker Miller, who showed the house to buyers and also made misrepresentations to them. The buyers sued the sellers for the misrepresentation. The sellers paid the judgment, then sued Miller, who, as their fiduciary, should have informed them of his misrepresentation. The court held that Miller was a subagent of the sellers because he had cooperated with the sellers' broker.

Example

In another case, *Walters v. Marker*, buyer Walters contacted agent Leseman, who worked with the seller's broker in the transaction. A court of appeal later held that "Leseman, as real estate agent of Walters, undeniably owed a fiduciary duty to buyer Walters. . . ."

■ Buyer's Broker

It is possible for a broker who does not have a specific property listed that the buyer is interested in to represent the buyer exclusively. This buyer's broker under the Civil Code is termed the "selling agent." Licensees operating in this capacity could enter into a Buyer-Broker Agreement.

■ Dual Agency

Agency law permits an agent to represent two principals but requires *disclosure* of the fact to both principals and the *consent* of both. An undisclosed dual agency violates the real estate law.

Duties in a Dual Agency Relationship

Once a dual agency has been established, the agent owes to *each* principal good faith, honesty, and loyalty to their mutual interests. The agent must respect and protect the confidentiality of information received from each principal and is prohibited from disclosing such information received from one principal to the other, without having the consent of the party from whom he or she received the information.

Probably the most common example of dual agency in real estate is escrow. The escrow handler represents both parties as a neutral third party and can carry out only the mutual or concurring instructions of seller and buyer or of lender and borrower.

Changing Roles

A licensee may be an agent of the seller during one stage of a transaction and an agent of the buyer during another stage.

Example

During escrow, the escrow holder was a dual agent representing the interests of both the buyer and the seller. After close of escrow, funds were withheld for completion of termite work. At this stage of the transaction, the escrow agent is now the agent of the buyer only and no longer a dual agent.

Commissions Do Not Determine Agency

The payment of compensation or the obligation to pay compensation to an agent by the seller or buyer does not necessarily define a particular agency relationship.

In addition, an arrangement to split a commission between agents does not necessarily establish an agency relationship. A listing agent and a selling agent may agree to share any compensation or commission that arises from a real estate transaction, but the terms of such an agreement do not define the agency relationship with the principal.

Example

A buyer engages a licensee to approach an owner and present an offer containing a provision for a seller-paid commission. The licensee may be found to be an agent of both seller and buyer unless the agreement clearly provides that the agent represents the buyer only and does not purport to have any kind of fiduciary relationship with the seller.

■ Unit 5 Review Quiz

1. An agent is eagerly trying to gain a buyer's loyalty before showing homes. He does not want to do a lot of work only to have the prospect run off with another agent. The buyer isn't sure about the agent's qualifications and ability to find the right home. The agent responds that his area of specialization is buyer brokerage. In addition, he says, "I am a member of the MLS, so I can access any available property in the market for you." This agent has violated his subagency duty to the sellers in the MLS.

   a. True

   b. False

2. A buyer's broker convinces the buyer to place an offer on one of her listings. Since the broker has fully informed her client that the property is her listing, she is no longer acting in a dual agency capacity.

   a. True

   b. False

3. A broker is trying to enter into a buyer-broker's agreement to represent a prospect. One of the broker's sales pitches is "you can have someone on your side, working for your interests, and it usually doesn't cost you anything because the seller pays the commission." This statement is not in violation of the laws of agency.

   a. True

   b. False

Breach of Duties

Once an agency relationship has been established, the licensee is bound to fiduciary and statutory duties. The agent's failure to perform such duties constitutes a "breach of duty." A breach can occur intentionally, negligently, or innocently.

■ Intentional Breach

When an agent intentionally commits a tortuous act, agency is not a defense. In other words, when a real estate licensee commits tortuous acts, the fact that the licensee is acting as an agent for another will not shield the agent from liability.

Example

A seller instructs an agent to sell unimproved property for residential purposes. The licensee does so, although both are aware that applicable zoning ordinances prohibit residential use. The fact that the seller instructed the licensee to represent the property as suitable for residential use would not exempt the licensee from liability for fraud.

Actual Fraud

Civil Code §1572 lists four types of actual fraud: false suggestion, false assertion, suppression, and false promises.

False suggestion.   A false suggestion is a false statement made by one *who does not believe it to be true.*

False assertion.   A false assertion is a false statement made by one *who has no reasonable ground for believing it to be true.*

Suppression.   Suppression is a failure to disclose a fact by one who is bound to disclose it, or who gives information of other facts that are likely to mislead.

False promises.   A false promise is promising something without any intention of performing it.

Constructive Fraud

Civil Code §1573 states that constructive fraud is any breach of duty that, without an actually fraudulent intent, gains an advantage for the person at fault by misleading another to his prejudice. This would include all acts, omissions, and concealments involving a breach of legal or equitable duty, trust, or confidence and resulting in damage to another.

Example

A buyer is about to make a 90 percent offer on a property. The buyer asks the selling agent if the offer is likely to be accepted, as the buyer really likes the property. The selling agent, who is acting as a dual agent, gives the buyer positive assurances, noting that the seller is in the middle of a long, contentious divorce. Sensing that the seller might have a cash problem, the buyer drops $10,000 off the price. The seller reluctantly accepts. At the closing, the buyer drops $10,000 off the price. The seller reluctantly accepts. After closing, the buyer tells the seller exactly what the agent had disclosed. Enraged, the seller sues the agent for breach of duty under the premise of constructive fraud.

Applicability to Real Estate Licensees

Licensees involved in fiduciary agency relationships are liable for constructive fraud. Further, a lack of fraudulent intent is no defense against a charge of constructive fraud. Therefore, it is imperative for a licensee to deal "above board" and document good faith efforts with appropriate letters, reports, and other memoranda whenever there is a possibility that the licensee may gain an advantage in the course of dealing with a principal.

■ Negligent Breach

Negligence is defined as the failure to do what a reasonable person would do under similar circumstances. The "reasonable person" standard is objective rather than subjective: the conduct required is the supposed conduct, under similar circumstances, of a hypothetical person representing a community ideal of reasonable behavior.

"Reasonable Person"

The "reasonable person" standard for licensees, against which a claim of negligence will be considered, is that of a real estate professional presumed to know more about real estate than the average person. Thus, the standard of knowledge, skill, and diligence for practitioners is a more demanding standard.

"Ideal Behavior"

The ideal conduct that forms the basis for determining the reasonableness of a licensee's conduct in a given situation may be established by statute or by the Commissioner's Regulations.

Special Expertise

If a licensee claims to have some particular skill greater than other licensees, and clients rely on that claim in choosing the licensee as their agent, the agent will be held to this higher standard and not just to the basic standard of other licensees.

A common example of the "higher standard" application occurs in the area of financial qualification. If agents obtain listings on the merits of their financial qualification skills, they had better do the job well. The liability is that an agent will qualify a buyer, assure the seller that the buyer is qualified, and then complete the sales contract. The home comes off the market for weeks, during which time numerous buyers are lost. If the buyer fails to qualify with the mortgage lender, the listing agent faces the liability of breaching fiduciary duty because of incompetence.

Reasonable Skill and Knowledge

In the absence of any representation as to special expertise, the standard of skill and knowledge required of a licensee is that which is commonly possessed by other practicing licensees of good standing in the same community. The standard is that which is common to those recognized in the profession itself as qualified and competent to engage in professional real estate activities.

Applicability to Real Estate Services

The "reasonable" standard of competence applies to all activities in which the licensee engages in the day-to-day operation of a real estate practice. Particularly applicable areas include:

- Advising the seller regarding property value
- Identifying which disclosures the seller should make to the buyer
- Advising buyers on matters of financing

In these and other everyday activities, the licensee will be expected to possess the knowledge and skill common to members of the profession.

Example

In *Ford v. Cournale,* a broker represented to a prospective buyer that an income property would yield a certain monthly income. The representation was based solely on the current owner's unverified statements. In fact, the monthly income failed to cover fixed expenses. The court held that since the broker purported to give advice and did so negligently, he could be held responsible for the damages.

Agency Is Not a Defense

As in situations involving intentional breach of duty, agency is not a defense against a licensee's liability for negligent torts committed against a third party.

Example

A broker holding an open house negligently places an object to hold a door open. If a visitor trips over the object and is injured, the broker is liable under general negligence principles. The fact that he was holding the open house as agent for the seller is no defense.

■ Innocent Breach

Courts have limited tort liability for innocent misrepresentations to cases involving property (real or personal) rather than sale of services. An innocent misrepresentation involved in the sale of services may, however, constitute a basis for rescission of a contract.

Tortuous Acts of Subagents

A subagent's tortuous acts may be considered "innocent" acts of the principal or agent, in that the principal or agent may not have been aware of or authorized such acts. If the subagency were authorized, the principal, and not the agent, is liable for the subagent's acts. If the principal did not authorize the subagency, the agent alone is liable. (Civil Code §§2350, 2351)

Example

A seller authorizes his broker to hire an advertising agency to help sell the house. Ordinarily, any misrepresentation by the advertising agency would subject the principal, and not the broker, to liability.

If the seller merely hired the broker to sell the house, and it was the broker's normal practice to obtain the advertising agency's assistance, any misstatement by the advertising agency would probably subject the broker, rather than the principal, to liability.

■ Unit 6 Review Quiz

1. A flood zone code prohibits ground-floor improvement of newly constructed homes. Numerous residents in the area improve these areas anyway, in violation of the code. One such resident lists his property with the advertisement that the home contains 2,000 SF of living area, inclusive of the ground floor recreation room. The listing agent represents to a buyer that the home has a wonderful extra room for the kids—which is why the listing price is a little higher than that of other similar homes. In this case, the agent has committed fraud.

   a. True
   b. False

2. A homeseller has just completed a new $30,000 septic system on his property. The system traverses a county road, a public easement that is hardly ever used due to the construction of another nearby road. In selling the property, the listing agent promotes the merits of the new septic system. After closing, the county informs the buyer that the system is illegal and must be moved away from the traversing easement—a ruling that will cost the buyers at least $25,000. The agent, however, is in the clear because she has disclosed the existence of the easement to the buyers.

   a. True
   b. False

3. A "waterfront specialist" listed a home on the Sacramento River with a 20-foot riverwall. There were vertical cracks in the wall, which a prospective buyer was quick to ask about. The agent told the buyers that vertical cracks were common, and that horizontal cracks were the ones to look out for—a well-known fact. After the closing, a flood caused six panels of the river wall to collapse. The buyers sued, but they had no real argument because the agent had openly discussed the cracks prior to closing.

   a. True
   b. False

4. A seller asks a prospective listing agent her opinion of what the property should list for. The agent knows similar properties in the area are selling for $150,000. Which is the best response?

   a. "I think we should hire an appraiser to give us that advice."
   b. "I think we should start at $170,000, then come down to $150,000."
   c. "I think we should run a CMA and go from there. It won't give us a complete story, but it's a start."
   d. "I think $170,000 is a good starting number, but let me do a CMA. That will tell us what the real value is."

Agency Relationships in Residential Transactions

The question "Whose agent are you?" has been a confusing one to many licensees, who are expected to understand the law of agency. It has been even more confusing and often misleading to the general public. In an effort to dispel this confusion and uncertainty, in January of 1988, the California legislature amended the Civil Code §§2079.13–2079.24. The following sections cover legal definitions and numerous important provisions of the code.

■ Disclosure Form Civil Code §2079.14

Listing agents and selling agents shall provide the seller and buyer in any nonexempt residential real property transaction with a copy of the disclosure form specified in Civil Code §2079.16 and, except as provided in subdivision (c), shall obtain a signed acknowledgment of receipt from that seller or buyer, except as provided in the Civil Code §2079.15, as follows:

Disclosure to Seller

The **listing agent**, if any, shall provide the disclosure form to the seller prior to entering into the listing agreement.

The **selling agent,** defined as the one who obtains a buyer for a property, shall provide the disclosure form to the seller as soon as practicable prior to presenting the seller with an offer to purchase, unless the selling agent previously provided the seller with a copy of the disclosure form.

Proper disclosure for the listing agent would be during the listing presentation and prior to the owner signing the listing agreement.

Disclosure at a distance. Where the selling agent does not deal on a face-to-face basis with the seller, the disclosure form may be furnished to the seller (and acknowledgment of receipt obtained for the selling agent from the seller) by the listing agent, or the selling agent may deliver the disclosure form by certified mail addressed to the seller at his or her last known address, in which case no signed acknowledgment of receipt is required.

Disclosure to Buyer

The **selling agent** shall provide the disclosure form to the buyer as soon as practicable prior to execution of the buyer's offer to purchase, except that if the offer to purchase is not prepared by the selling agent, the selling agent shall present the disclosure form to the buyer not later than the next business day after the selling agent receives the offer to purchase from the buyer.

■ Refusal to Acknowledge Civil Code §2079.15

In any circumstances in which the seller or buyer refuses to sign an acknowledgment of receipt of the disclosure form, the agent, or an associate licensee acting for an agent, shall set forth, sign, and date a written declaration of the facts of the refusal.

■ Agency Disclosures Civil Code §2079.17

(A) Selling Agent Disclosures

As soon as practicable, the selling agent shall disclose to the buyer and seller whether the selling agent is acting in the real property transaction exclusively as the buyer's agent, exclusively as the seller's agent, or as a dual agent representing both the buyer and the seller.

This relationship shall be confirmed in the contract to purchase and sell real property or in a separate writing executed or acknowledged by the seller, the buyer, and the selling agent prior to or coincident with execution of that contract by the buyer and the seller, respectively.

(B) Listing Agent Disclosures

As soon as practicable, the listing agent shall disclose to the seller whether the listing agent is acting in the real property transaction exclusively as the seller's agent or as a dual agent representing both the buyer and seller. This relationship shall be confirmed in the contract to purchase and sell real property or in a separate writing executed or acknowledged by the seller and the listing agent prior to or coincident with the execution of that contract by the seller.

(C) Confirmation Requirements

The confirmation required by 2079.17 shall be in the following form:

_____ (Name of Listing Agent) is the agent of (check one):
❑ the seller exclusively   ❑ both the buyer and seller
_____ (Name of the Selling Agent if not the same as the Listing Agent) is the agent of (check one):
❑ the buyer exclusively   ❑ the seller exclusively   ❑ both the buyer and seller

Prohibited Disclosures by Dual Agent Civil Code §2079.21

A dual agent shall not disclose to the buyer that the seller is willing to sell the property at a price less than the listing price, without the express written consent of the seller.

A dual agent shall not disclose to the seller that the buyer is willing to pay a price greater than the offering price, without the express written consent of the buyer.

This section does not alter in any way the duty or responsibility of a dual agent to any principal with respect to confidential information other than price.

Example

Consider a dual agency situation where the seller has disclosed to the agent that his business is going very poorly and the cash flow situation is terrible. The seller encourages the agent to find a buyer, even if it means dropping the price. The dual agent is prohibited from conveying this information to any buyer, since nothing was put in writing. Moreover, the agent would violate confidentiality by disclosing the seller's business problems. If asked, "personal reasons" is a good response.

Agents May Be Selling and Listing Agents Civil Code §2079.22

Nothing in the law precludes a listing agent from also being a selling agent, and the combination of these functions in one agent does not, of itself, make that agent a dual agent.

A selling agent is not the same as a buyer's agent. Rather, the term refers to the agent responsible for obtaining the buyer. If a buyer wishes no representation—represents himself—then the listing agent is the one responsible for selling the house and therefore both the listing and selling agent, although not a dual agent.

Agency Relationship Is Changeable by Mutual Consent Civil Code §2079.23

A contract between the principal and agent may be modified or altered to change the agency relationship at any time before the performance of the act that is the object of the agency, with the written consent of the parties to the agency relationship.

Agency Disclosure and Confirmation

There has been tremendous confusion regarding the terms "disclosure" and "confirmation," two very different steps in the agency disclosure process that must be given to the principals at different times during the real estate transaction. In fact, even the appellate courts have confused the meaning of these terms.

The term "agency disclosure" really should be called "agency education" because the agency disclosure form (CAR Standard Form AD) is a statutorily defined form that educates the seller and the buyer as to the duties and responsibilities of a listing agent, selling agent, and dual agent. Its purpose is NOT to select who is representing whom. The function of the "agency confirmation" paragraph in the purchase agreement or the "agency confirmation" form (CAR Standard Form AC-6) is to inform the seller and buyer as to who is representing whom and whether or not an office is acting as a dual agent in this particular transaction.

Q.1. To what transactions does the agency disclosure law apply?

A. It applies to sales, exchanges, and leases for more than one year, involving real property improved with one to four dwelling units, stock cooperatives, and mobile homes. The law applies whether the property is owner-occupied or not.

Q.2 How do licensees comply with the requirement to provide the written agency disclosure form to both the seller and the buyer?

A. Listing agent—must provide this form to the seller prior to entering into a listing agreement.

Selling agent—must provide this form to the buyer as soon as practicable prior to the execution of the buyer's offer to purchase. In fact, the form should be provided to the buyer as soon as that buyer seeks the services of the agent in more than a "casual, transitory, or preliminary manner," with the object of entering into a real property transaction.

In addition, the selling agent must provide the disclosure form to the seller as soon as practicable prior to presenting the seller with an offer.

In other words, both the listing agent and the selling agent must provide the seller with separate disclosure forms. Therefore, in a transaction with two different offices, the seller will receive two disclosure forms, while the buyer will only receive one disclosure form (from the selling agent).

If the same office represents both sides, the buyer and seller will each receive only one form. Each time a client receives a disclosure form, he or she should sign it acknowledging receipt and give a copy to the licensee who gave it to him or her.

Q.3 How and when does the confirmation of the agency relationships take place?

A. Both the listing agent (office) and selling agent (office) must "elect" (i.e., choose) which form of agency representation they desire as soon as practicable. These relationships must then be "confirmed" either in one or more statutorily defined agency confirmation forms or in a purchase contract that includes the statutorily defined agency confirmation language.

Note that different salespersons or broker-associates with one firm cannot have different agency relationships with a principal. All licensees within a firm must represent the same parties in a transaction. In other words, the office/firm is the agent for the principal.

Q.4 Which agency disclosure forms does a listing or selling agent have to keep in his or her files?

A. The listing agent and selling agent must keep for three years all documents signed by the agent or obtained by the agent in connection with any real estate transaction.

Unit 7 Review Quiz

1. In effect, the selling agent does not have to present an agency disclosure form to the seller, since that is the listing agent's responsibility.

   a. True

   b. False

2. A selling agent is careful to disclose his agency relationship to a prospective buyer. After two weeks of negotiation with a seller, the buyer places an offer on a property, at which time the agent informs the seller that he represents the buyer. In this case, the selling agent

   a. has properly disclosed the agency to the buyer, but improperly to the seller.

   b. has property disclosed to the seller, but improperly to the buyer.

   c. has properly disclosed the agency to both parties.

   d. has improperly disclosed the agency to both parties.

3. An agent is disclosed as a dual agent in an impending transaction. The listing price is $200,000. The buyer asks the agent what she should offer. The agent replies, "Well, the average accepted offer in our market has recently been about 90 percent of the listing price. So an offer of $180,000 would be considered a serious offer." Here, the agent has not violated his duty as a dual agent.

   a. True

   b. False

Definitions Civil Code Section 2079.13

As used in this section, the following terms have the following meanings:

Agent

A person acting under provisions of this title in a real property transaction, including a person who is licensed as a real estate broker and under whose license a listing is executed or an offer to purchase is obtained.

Associate Licensee

A licensed broker or salesperson working under a broker's supervision as the broker's agent in connection with acts requiring a real estate license.

When an associate licensee owes a duty to any principal or third party, that duty is equivalent to the duty owed to that party by the broker for whom the associate licensee functions.

Buyer

A transferee in a real property transaction, including a person who executes an offer to purchase real property from a seller through an agent, or who seeks the services of an agent in more than a casual, transitory, or preliminary manner, with the object of entering into a real property transaction. "Buyer" includes vendee or lessee.

Dual Agent

An agent acting, either directly or through an associate licensee, as agent for both the seller and the buyer in a real property transaction.

Note: Although this is the code definition, there is some confusion. While it is common to call salespeople "agents," it is a misnomer. The agent is the brokerage not the licensee. This can create complications, such as in the case where a buyer and a seller were being represented by two different salespeople from the same real estate firm. There would still be dual agency.

Listing Agreement

A contract between an owner of real property and an agent, by which the agent has been authorized to sell the real property or to find or obtain a buyer.

Listing Agent

A person who has obtained a listing of real property to act as an agent for compensation.

Listing Price

The amount expressed in dollars specified in the listing for which the seller is willing to sell the real property through the listing agent.

Offering Price

The amount expressed in dollars specified in an offer to purchase for which the buyer is willing to buy the real property.

Offer to Purchase

A written contract executed by a buyer acting through a selling agent that becomes the contract for the sale of the real property upon acceptance by the seller.

Real Property

Any estate . . . in property which constitutes or is improved with one to four dwelling units, any leasehold in this type of property exceeding one year's duration, and mobile homes, when offered for sale or sold through [a licensed real estate] agent. . . .

Real Property Transaction

A transaction for the sale of real property in which an agent is employed by one or more of the principals to act in that transaction, including a listing or an offer to purchase.

"Sell," "Sale," or "Sold"

A transaction for the transfer of real property from the seller to the buyer, including exchanges . . . real property sales contract . . . [and] creation of a leasehold exceeding one year's duration.

Seller

The transferor in a real property transaction, including an owner who lists real property with an agent, whether or not a transfer results, or who receives an offer to purchase real property, of which he or she is the owner, from an agent on behalf of another. "Seller" includes both a vendor and a lessor.

Selling Agent

A selling agent can be a listing agent who acts alone. It can also be an agent who acts in cooperation with a listing agent and who sells or finds and obtains a buyer for the real property. A selling agent can also be an agent who locates property for a buyer or who finds a buyer for a property for which no listing exists and presents an offer to purchase to the seller.

Subagent

A person to whom an agent delegates agency powers. . . . However, "subagent" does not include an associate licensee who is acting under the supervision of an agent in a real property transaction.

Unit 1 Review Answers

1. **b.** The laws of agency apply to all agency relationships, not merely to those in real estate brokerage.

Unit 2 Review Answers

1. **d.** The brother may seek buyers, as such activity falls within the scope of authority granted by the power of attorney.
2. **a.** By accepting the benefits of the agent's actions, the seller may have created an agency relationship by ratification. "Ratification normally results when the purported agent has held himself or herself out as representing the principal, and the principal then accepts the benefits of the purported agent's actions." The signed purchase contract is a writing that confirms that the commission is payable, so the statute of frauds requirements would be met.
3. **a.** Even though the agency agreement was not in writing, the seller accepted a purchase agreement containing provisions for payment of a commission. Therefore, the agent can enforce payment under the terms of the agreement.
4. **b.** The agent may pursue legal remedies to recover unreimbursed expenses, despite the fact that the relationship is terminated.
5. **a.** Civil Code §2330 states that the acts of the agent are the acts of the principal when the agent is acting within the scope of the agency. Ordering a termite treatment would not be construed as within the scope of a management agreement. Therefore, the principal is not liable for the unauthorized acts of his or her agent beyond the scope of authority. The agent will have to pay the bill.
6. **a.** Since the franchise requires the licensee to use the company's methodology for analyzing markets, and since the person keeps regular office hours at the company, the person would most likely be considered an employee, regardless of the compensation structure.

Unit 3 Review Answers

1. **b.** All the agent's actions must be aimed at accomplishing for the principal the purpose for which the agent was employed. It is improper, without disclosure, for an agent to act for his or her own benefit in an agency situation.
2. **a.** The broker has disclosed his listing in the subdivision and his agency relationship with the buyers, and has made it clear he stands to profit from their purchase in the new subdivision. By showing the buyer client his listings first, he has fulfilled his duty to his subdivider principal.
3. **a.** The listing agent may have been negligent in failing to conduct a competitive market analysis if in fact other agents in the market are so doing. It is likely that the property was underpriced, as evidenced by the quick sale and the apparently superior knowledge of the buyers. If this turns

out to be true, and the seller relied on the "expertise" of the agent, the agent could be liable for failing to meet the appropriate standard of care.

4. **b.** Agent Bill bears liability for breaching the duty to investigate material facts impacting the transaction, in this case, mechanics' liens. If a court finds this failure to be beneath the local standard of care, the agent is negligent. If there were a buyer's broker involved, he or she would be liable as well.

Unit 4 Review Answers

1. **d.** First, the agent should exercise caution not to misrepresent the cause of foundation cracks. It might be settling, earthquakes, land movement, or some other cause. He should advise the buyers to seek an expert opinion. Second, agents in San Mateo should know where the San Andreas Fault is—unless they want to conceal facts they ought to be disclosing.

Unit 5 Review Answers

1. **b.** The agent has clearly represented himself as a potential agent for the buyer, since buyer brokers represent buyers. In itself, accessing MLS properties does not create subagency, because the buyer broker can disclose whom he represents to any individual seller or listing agent. In so doing, he refuses any offer of subagency implicit in the MLS.
2. **b.** Having disclosed and obtained consent for the dual agency with the buyer, the broker has eliminated the problem of nondisclosure with the buyer. The broker must also inform the seller of the dual representation and obtain the seller's consent.
3. **a.** The agent has not violated agency law. The question of who pays agent compensation does not of itself determine agency or where one's fiduciary duty lies. It is not unusual in residential and commercial brokerage for the seller to pay all or part of the buyer representative's commission through a commission split with the listing agent.

Unit 6 Review Answers

1. **a.** The agent has suppressed the code violation that could lead to serious problems in the future. The agent has further made the false assertion that, since the home has a recreation room, it is worth more than other homes that have presumably conformed to code. To avoid the problem, the agent should disclose the code violation and refrain from associating such a violation with an increase in value.
2. **b.** The agent is clearly liable for constructive fraud. She omitted to inform the buyers that there was not only an easement, but that the septic system encroached upon it illegally. While the agent may not have intended the omission, lack of intent is no defense in her case.
3. **b.** The buyers in fact have a good claim. The agent, a "specialist" on waterfront property, had told them not to worry, and they relied on this "expert" advice, which proved to be quite wrong. If the agent is to reap the benefits of being a waterfront expert, he must also face the consequences of incompetence.
4. **c.** The agent has wisely suggested researching the value prior to identifying any numbers. She has also cautioned the seller that the CMA only gives an indication, and that it is not an appraisal.

Unit 7 Review Answers

1. **b.** It is the selling agent's responsibility to provide the disclosure form to the seller prior to presenting an offer.

2. **a.** The early disclosure to the buyer was proper, but the seller must be informed "as soon as is practicable." Since the agent had two weeks to make the disclosure, one could argue that a "practicable" opportunity had been ignored.

3. **a.** The agent did not say that the seller would accept $180,000, only that by market standards such an offer reflected the actual difference between listing and selling prices. By objective standards, therefore, 90 percent offers are indeed "serious offers."

Course 2: Ethics

Introduction to Ethics

Ethics is the name we give to our concern for good behavior. We feel an obligation to consider not only our own personal well-being, but also that of others and of human society as a whole.

You can easily determine whether a course of action is ethical simply by asking, "Would I want someone else to act in this manner toward me?" This, of course, is known as the Golden Rule and is the cornerstone of the NAR Code of Ethics. Most people coming into real estate do not enter the business to do it unethically. Unfortunately, however, it doesn't take very long to realize that the only way to get paid in this business is to close the escrow. Therefore, you direct your activities and behavior to do whatever it takes to get the listing and close the escrow. This may result in little regard for your responsibilities to your sellers, your buyers, and fellow licensees.

Professional ethics are rules or standards governing the conduct of a profession. Professional associations define and enforce these standards, which typically address education and training, standards of competence, service to the community, and the profession's good name.

Governments also regulate professions, both through the general civil and criminal laws that apply to all personal and business conduct, and through special laws and administrative regulations applying to particular professions and industries.

Most laws today are based on ethical behavior. Even though the two are separate, the realms of law and ethics overlap. Also, many times where laws end is where ethics begins. For example, there is no law per se regarding "stealing" clients/customers, but it is certainly unethical behavior. Conduct that is "right" is probably both legal and ethical according to accepted codes, and conduct that is intuitively perceived as "wrong" is probably prohibited by both law and ethics. However, there are gray areas where conduct considered by a profession or by the public to be unethical is not specifically forbidden by the law.

■ The Department of Real Estate (DRE)

In California, the Department of Real Estate licenses individuals to practice the profession of real estate and regulates their conduct through the power to suspend or revoke licenses for illegal conduct or to put licensees on restriction or probation.

Most laws having to do with real estate licensees' conduct are found in the California Business and Professions Code and the DRE's regulations, which are found in the Code of Regulations. These laws and regulations apply to all brokers and salespersons licensed by the state of California.

■ DRE's Major Concerns

The four major ethical concerns of the Department of Real Estate are:

1. Conflict of interest
2. Misrepresentation of positive features of a property
3. Nondisclosure of negative features
4. Mishandling of clients' funds

Conflict of Interest

Conflict of interest is one of the principal complaints leading to suspension or revocation of licenses. A conflict of interest occurs when an agent violates or evades the fiduciary relationship by such actions as fraudulent conduct, dual representation without disclosure, failure to disclose a financial interest in a transaction, undisclosed special relationships with buyer or seller, and commingling of funds.

Concealing secret profits. Trying to make a secret profit on a principal's transaction is an obvious violation of the agency relationship. It could take many forms. Purchasing property for yourself with the obvious intention of reselling it to a buyer at a much higher price is one example. Some companies will not allow their sales associates to purchase office listings for resale. The purpose here is to avoid the appearance of a conflict of interest. If a property is underpriced, the agent has a duty to tell the owner. The appearance of unethical self-dealing reflects negatively on the firm and the entire real estate industry.

Another area is utilization of ancillary services for a customer/client without disclosing that you will in some way benefit by the referral. In other words, an agent starts to shake hands with the palm up instead of straight up with the palm sideways. A major property management firm in California was reprimanded by the DRE when it was discovered that it was billing its clients at the retail rate for advertising vacancies when in fact it was paying a wholesale rate based on its volume of advertising.

Concealing a hidden profit is an obvious conflict of interest. A conflict, however, may also be unintentional. In the recent case of *Blackburn v. McCoy*, a licensee sold a property where other associates in his office were receiving a secret profit without his knowledge. The licensee was acquitted of any wrongdoing, but it took a court trial to clear him of liability.

Misrepresentation vs. Puffing

Over the years, the courts have addressed the fine distinction between misrepresentation and mere sales talk known as embellishing.

What distinguishes one from the other, as defined by court decisions, is whether a reasonable person would have relied on the statement. "Spectacular, gated dream home…" may be stretching the terms a bit when we are talking about a remodeled fixer home with a gate and fence in the front yard. Certainly, the terms "spectacular" and "dream home" are very subjective and do not necessarily constitute misrepresentation.

Increasing liability for misrepresentation. Misrepresentation by an agent can come about in two ways: making a false statement of fact (commission) OR failing to disclose a material fact (omission). The old days of keeping your fingers crossed and saying to yourself, "I hope this buyer doesn't ask why this area is called 'San Andreas Estate,'" are gone. Agents have a nice way of protecting themselves from misinformation about a property by requesting/requiring a property inspection. This does not relieve them, however, of a duty to disclose information that they should be informed about (about a neighborhood, for example) because they are "in the business." The seller may have imparted information to the agent that affects the desirability of a property.

Agents over recent years have become increasingly liable for making misrepresentations. The following cases are representative:

- A salesperson had indicated that there was only one trust deed on a property, although there were two, and *was not* held liable since he had no knowledge of the second lien.

- An agent who represented the availability of well water on a property for sale *was* held liable because he had personal knowledge that the facts were other than as represented.

Failure to Disclose Material Facts Affecting Value

The courts have been sympathetic to consumers where failure to be completely truthful distorts value.

Also, they have ruled that the licensee has some obligation to investigate as well as disclose adverse factors reasonably apparent to someone with real estate expertise. The Transfer Disclosure Statement (now 20 years old) set out to remedy most of the nondisclosure problems. The agent still needs to make a visual inspection of the readily accessible areas to determine anything that affects the value or desirability of the property.

Example

The complainant, a member of the public and a licensee with access to the MLS purchased a property that had been listed by respondents A and B. The listing included a 3,948-square-foot home on a 49,522-square-foot lot with over 40 fruit and palm trees.

After listing, the respondents found that the property was actually two different adjacent parcels owned by the same party. The respondent changed the MLS listing but did not change the description, which read,

"Great landscaping w/over 40 fruit and palm trees." If fact, the trees were actually on the adjacent, unimproved property and not part of the listed property.

Nine days after the buyers offer was accepted, the seller sent a letter saying that a fence would be erected to separate the two parcels that would result in a "slight change to configuration of the driveway of the purchased property." During the next three weeks, the buyer tried to get a definition from the seller and respondents of what a "slight change to the driveway really meant." Through testimony, it was determined that the respondents had knowledge detailing the problem and had a survey map in their possession, but they would not give it for fear of jeopardizing the close of escrow. Respondents were found to be in violation of Article 1 for failing to treat all parties fairly and honestly and for misrepresenting the property being sold, exaggerating the amenities, and concealing the impact of the encroachment problem.

Example

In another case, the plaintiff charged that the salesperson had represented that a home's foundation was sound, when in fact the house was infested with wood-destroying fungus. The court found that the plaintiff had indeed been damaged by this nondisclosure.

Mishandling of Funds

One of the mandatory courses for the renewal of all licensees is "Trust Fund Handling." This term includes everything from forgetting to enter money received from a customer into a trust fund journal to walking around town with a deposit check and outright misuse of customer funds for a personal use (known as conversion). This separate course goes far beyond what is covered in an ethics course.

■ Professional Organizations

In addition to government regulation by law, professional associations, through their power to grant or withhold membership, also regulate real estate ethics. Membership requirements typically include adherence to a code of ethics.

Professional organizations address aspects of ethics, public service, and professionalism that are not strictly within the realm of law. The possibility of censure or expulsion by one's peers discourages unethical conduct.

For California licensees, the most widely known and followed code is that of the National Association of REALTORS®. Other professional associations have their own codes. These include the National Association of Real Estate Brokers (Realtists), the California Escrow Association, and the Appraisal Institute.

CAR's Ethical Concerns

Before anyone can join the California Association of REALTORS®, he or she must join a local association that requires an indoctrination of all new members. It covers things like antitrust activities, which could involve everything from boycotting certain brokers because of the discounting of brokerage fees to fixing prices/commissions. In addition, one has to pledge to do business according the NAR Code of Ethics and Standards of Practice set forth in the code.

The California Association of Realtors® reports three principal areas of concern over violations of NAR's Code of Ethics:

1. Conflict of interest
2. Misrepresentation or concealment of facts
3. Advertising

Concerns of Local Associations

Local associations of Realtors® have their own distinctive concerns and procedures. These include:

- Multiple listing violations
- Favored access to information
- Pressure for income in hard times
- Disciplinary powers

Multiple Listing Violations

Multiple listing services are designed to provide maximum exposure for the client and equal opportunities for licensees.

In a "hot" market, members will withhold listings from the multiple listing service over the prescribed presentation period (typically 48 hours) in order to get both listing and selling commissions.

Pocket listings—again bypassing the multiple listing service—keep properties off the MLS by having sellers sign a document authorizing this. The unethical licensee induces the owner to sign by saying that it is somehow in their best interest "so you won't have a bunch of unqualified buyers going through your house and we can truly give you professional service…."

Relisting a property as if there is a change to avoid the appearance of a stale listing is another violation, as is failure to treat all parties honestly.

Example

The complainant, Realtor A, alleged that the respondent, Realtor B, paged her on a Saturday to inform her that he had an offer on her listing. Realtor A replied that the owner was out of town and would be available to hear his offer two days later on Monday. When Realtor A arrived on Sunday to host an open house, she found the key to the door was missing. She contacted Realtor B immediately to bring the key to her, and he said he did not have it. He later phoned that he had mistakenly given the key to his buyer. He did return it but not in time for her to host her open house. Realtor B was found to be in violation of keybox regulations of the MLS.

Favored Access to Information

Some members, because of local association politics, may have access to listings that have not yet reached the multiple listing book and may work on them before other members know of their existence, giving themselves almost the same advantage as that of the listing broker.

Pressure for Income in Hard Times

The temptation to "create" transactions in slow periods can be overwhelming. It is a time for particular caution with regard to anything that might be perceived as self-dealing, deception, or overstated advertising.

Disciplinary Powers

Most local associations of REALTORS® have standing committees to handle complaints made by the public or member licensees. An accused agent will have to go before a committee of peers to answer for his or her behavior. The result of this hearing will either be a dismissal, letter of censure, or outright loss of membership in the organization. This will occur particularly when there are repeated violations of association rules and bylaws.

As as example, a broker in the San Fernando Valley was terminated from membership in the association for not supervising his sales personnel. He had over 300 licensees in his office, one part-time secretary, and no office manager. Needless to say, his agents were repeatedly causing problems with clients, customers, and other licensees—no training or sales meeting were ever held in his office!

■ Unit 1 Review Quiz

1. The laws and regulations of the Department of Real Estate apply to all real estate licensees.

    (a.) True

    b. False

2. Which ethical violation is one of the most common causes of license suspensions and revocations?

    a. Puffing

    b. Concealing hidden profits

    (c.) Conflict of interest

    d. Nondisclosure of fungus

3. The California Association of REALTORS® is primarily concerned about violations of the multiple listing service.

    (a.) True

    b. False

Sale, Lease, and Exchange Transactions: Unlawful Conduct

The real estate law defines and prohibits unlawful acts and omissions in the following areas of sale, lease, and exchange transactions:

- Misrepresenting market value
- Existence of offers
- Negotiability of commissions
- Broker affiliation
- Closing costs
- Deposits
- Buyer's qualifications
- Unauthorized changes
- Misrepresenting security value
- Misrepresenting the condition of property
- Misrepresenting size and boundaries
- Concealing use restrictions
- Nondisclosure of material facts
- Failing to present offers
- Bias in presenting competing offers
- Not explaining contingencies
- Nondisclosure of agent's interest
- Interest in referrals

■ Misrepresenting Market Value

Real estate law prohibits knowingly making a substantial misrepresentation of the likely value of real property to an owner or buyer for the purpose of:

- Securing a listing. This practice is known as highballing. Agents know that sellers want to hear the highest price for their property (even though it is not a realistic price). When asked why they would knowingly take an overpriced listing, agents give a dozen reasons, from "He can always come down; I want my For Sale sign in this neighborhood" to "I get lunch with the manager and win the monthly listing contest!"
- Acquiring an interest in the property for the licensee's own account.
- Inducing the buyer to make an offer to purchase the real property.

Example

In an actual case, a seller wanted to list his property for sale at $13,000. His broker advised him to list it at $12,000, stating that this was the appraised value. Later, the broker advised the seller to reduce the price to $10,000, explaining that he couldn't find buyers at the listed price. Meanwhile, the broker produced an offer of $10,000 from a buyer with whom he was associated and negotiated a sale to a third party for $13,500, without telling the original seller, his client. The seller compromised at a price of $10,250, and the broker consummated both sales concurrently. The real estate commissioner revoked the broker's license.

■ Existence of Offers

Real estate law prohibits a licensee who is seeking a listing from an owner of real property from representing to the owner that the licensee has obtained a bona fide written offer to purchase the property unless the licensee is in fact in possession of a bona fide written offer to purchase at the time of the representation.

Example

A prospective purchaser enters the office of a real estate broker, inquiring about the availability of housing in a particular development. The broker contacts Mr. and Mrs. Lester, who own a residence in the same development, and tells them that he has an offer to purchase their house at a most favorable price from a very qualified buyer. The broker induces the Lesters to list with him, even though he does not have a firm offer.

Negotiability of Commissions

The perception of the public is that commissions in real estate are pretty much set in concrete. CBS's *60 Minutes* ran a segment in May 2007 saying that 6 percent was the going commission on residential properties and that brokers who charged less than that amount had their listings shunned by MLS members.

In fact, real estate law prohibits a licensee from stating or implying to an owner of real property during listing negotiations that the licensee cannot accept less than the quoted commission or fee because of a law, regulation, or the rules of any organization other than the broker firm seeking the listing.

Business and Professions Code §10147.5 further provides that any printed listing agreement for the sale of real property consisting of four or fewer residential units must contain a notice in *ten-point boldface type* that the amount of the commission is not fixed by law and may be negotiable between seller and broker.

Example

A homeseller is interviewing a number of real estate salespeople, trying to decide which one to list his home with. The seller mentions to each one that he is willing to pay a commission of 5 percent and asks if that would be acceptable. Two of the salespeople reply that their brokers require a commission of 6 percent, while the third states that the California Association of REALTORS® requires its members to charge a commission of 6 percent. The third salesperson is in violation of the regulation.

■ Broker Affiliation

Real estate law prohibits knowingly making substantial misrepresentations regarding the licensee's relationship with an individual broker, corporate broker, or franchised brokerage company or that entity's or person's responsibility for the licensee's activities.

Example

Implying to prospective sellers that it is better to do business with a brokerage because it is a member of a national franchise is prohibited. The implication is that the national franchise organization will stand behind any transaction, which is not the case. The phrase "each office is independently owned and operated" means there is no franchise guarantee as to the success or problems that may arise in any transaction.

■ Closing Costs

It is unlawful as well as unethical to knowingly underestimate the closing costs of a transaction to a prospective buyer of seller. This practice is known as "lowballing" a client. The purpose here is to induce a person to make or accept an offer to purchase property.

Example

A broker avoids discussing the subject of closing costs with either the buyer or the seller on the theory that everyone knows that there will be closing costs in a real estate transaction, so it should not be necessary to disclose something that is well known and obvious. Further, the broker believes that neither a buyer nor a seller should make decisions based primarily on a minor consideration like closing costs. This broker has violated real estate law.

■ Deposits

Real estate law prohibits knowingly making a false or misleading representation to the seller of real property as to the form, amount, or treatment of a deposit toward the purchase of the property made by an offeror.

Example

An agent prepares a deposit receipt for the purchase of real property and acknowledges receipt of $1,000 from the buyer. The buyer does not have a checking account, but does have money on deposit in a savings account.

The agent suggests that the buyer sign a demand promissory note for $1,000 but fails to inform the seller of the form of payment at the time the offer to purchase is presented.

■ Buyer's Qualifications

Real estate law prohibits knowingly making a false or misleading representation to a seller of real property who has agreed to finance all or part of a purchase price by carrying back a loan about a buyer's ability to repay the loan in accordance with its terms and conditions.

Example

A seller is asked to take back a second trust deed in the sale of a residence, primarily because the buyer may not qualify conventionally. The broker is aware of the marginal condition of the buyer. Nevertheless, the broker assures the seller in no uncertain terms that the buyer is qualified and will make the necessary payments. The broker has violated real estate law.

■ Unauthorized Changes

Real estate law prohibits making an addition to or modification of the terms of an instrument previously signed or initialed by a party to a transaction without the knowledge and consent of the party.

Example

If a licensee changes or modifies a document previously signed, this act may be in excess of his or her authority as agent and might perpetrate a fraud upon the principal(s) concerned.

■ Misrepresenting Security Value

Real estate law prohibits making a representation as a principal or agent to a prospective purchaser of a promissory note secured by real property about the market value of the securing property without a reasonable basis for believing the truth and accuracy of the representation.

Example

A licensee tells a home equity lender that a certain house whose owner he represents has a market value of $300,000, when the licensee has performed no recent comparative market analysis and seen no qualified appraisal on the property. When a property will be the security for a note secured by a trust deed or mortgage, the fair market value is a material fact to a prospective investor in the note.

■ Misrepresenting the Condition of Property

Real estate law prohibits knowingly making a false or misleading representation, or a representation without a reasonable basis for believing its truth, concerning the nature or condition of the features of a property when soliciting an offer.

Example

Seller A came to realtor B's office explaining that his company was transferring him and he needed to sell his house. In the listing contract, seller A specified that the house had hardwood floors throughout and the price would include the shutters and drapes that were custom-made. Seller A said he would like to occupy the house for 90 days while his wife looked for another location. Realtor B advertised the house, showed it to a number of prospective buyers, and obtained a purchase contract from buyer C.

When C moved in, seeing the house for the first time in its unfurnished condition, he observed that the hardwood flooring existed only on the outer rim of the floor in each room that had been visible beyond the edges of rugs when he inspected the house. Each room had subflooring material under the carpets. Seller A later said it was a cost-cutting measure when he built the house and had simply forgotten about it. Realtor B was found to have acted in good faith but still had to endure the cost of going through a lawsuit by buyer C. Moral: Don't advertise something unless you are absolutely sure of the facts.

■ Misrepresenting Size and Boundaries

Real estate law prohibits knowingly making a false or misleading representation, or a representation without a reasonable basis for believing its truth, of the size of a parcel, square footage of improvements, or the location of the boundary lines of real property being offered for sale, lease, or exchange.

Example

A listing place with a multiple listing service leaves blank the spaces for the square footage of the dwelling and the dimensions of the lot. A licensee does not take measurements or otherwise obtain reliable figures, but tells a prospective buyer that the lot size is at least one acre because that is what the zoning requires it to be.

■ Concealing Use Restrictions

Real estate law prohibits knowingly making a false or misleading representation, or a representation without a reasonable basis to believe its truth, that a property can be used for certain purposes with the intent of inducing the prospective buyer or lessee to acquire an interest in the real property.

Example

A buyer entered into a contract to buy an undeveloped lot that was next to a Caltrans equipment facility, intending to build a ministorage building. He specifically asked the salesperson if Caltrans had any interest in the parcel, and the salesperson said Caltrans had none. However, the salesperson had firsthand knowledge that Caltrans did have an interest, and apparently the seller did also. The seller refused to hold the buyer's title company harmless against any condemnation action by the state, so the buyer refused to close escrow. The state filed eminent domain proceedings and took possession of the lot. After the dust of suits and countersuits had cleared, the seller's broker and salesperson owed the buyer $1 million "lost profits" plus expenditures and punitive damages. They were also in danger of having their licenses suspended or revoked.

■ Nondisclosure of Material Facts

Real estate law prohibits failing to disclose to a prospective purchaser or lessee facts that materially affect the value or desirability of the property, when the licensee knows the facts and has reason to believe that such facts are not known to and are not readily observable by a prospective purchaser or lessee.

Example

Realtor A was asked to list a neglected house that obviously needed a wide range of repairs. He strongly advised the owner that it would be to his advantage to put the house in good repair before offering it for sale, but the owner wanted it sold "as is." Realtor A wrote a novel advertisement offering a "clunker" in poor condition as a challenge to an ambitious do-it-yourself hobbyist.

A few days later, sales associate B showed the house to a retired couple who had been attracted by the ad because the husband was looking forward to applying his fix-up hobby to improving a home. The sale was made. Shortly thereafter, realtor A was charged with misrepresenting the condition of the property. Realtor A showed up at the hearing with sales associate B and a copy of the candid advertisement. The buyer understood the house was in poor condition but while inspecting the property, sales associate B commented that since the house was made of concrete block and stucco construction, there would not be termite worries. However, after the sale was made, the buyer ripped out a sill to replace it and found it swarming with termites with damage to the floors also in evidence. Realtor A had to pay for the cost of exterminating the building and the cost of lumber to repair damage because of B's failure to recommend a termite inspection. Realtor A was held responsible for the errors and misstatements made by the sales associate.

■ Failing to Present Offers

Real estate law prohibits willfully failing to present or cause to be presented to the owner of the property any written offer to purchase received prior to the closing of a sale, unless expressly instructed by the owner not to present such an offer, or unless the offer is patently frivolous.

Example

The listing price of a property for sale is $200,000, but the seller has not indicated to the listing agent any minimum acceptable price. The agent receives a written offer of $100,000 cash. Is this 50 percent offer frivolous? It is not for the agent to decide. The agent must present the offer.

■ Bias in Presenting Competing Offers

Real estate law prohibits presenting competing written offers to purchase real property to the owner in such a manner as to induce the owner to accept the offer that will provide the greatest compensation to the listing broker without regard to the benefits, advantages, or disadvantages to the owner.

Example

A salesperson representing the seller of a property receives two offers on the same day. One is a full-price offer with no contingencies. The other is a 90 percent offer contingent on the obtaining of suitable financing. The salesperson presents the full-price offer, knowing it will be accepted, and withholds the 90 percent offer. In effect, the salesperson has made a decision about the offers that should be made by the seller, as well as helping himself to a larger commission.

■ Not Explaining Contingencies

Real estate law prohibits failing to explain to the parties or prospective parties to a real estate transaction for whom the licensee is acting as an agent the meaning and probable significance of a contingency in an offer or contract that the licensee knows or reasonably believes may affect the closing date of the transaction, or the timing of the vacating of the property by the seller or its occupancy by the buyer.

Any statement by the agent to the seller ensuring the closing of escrow within the specified period without first explaining to the seller the significance of the contingency would be a violation.

Example

A buyer makes an offer to purchase a property that includes a contingency that the buyer has to close the sale of her current residence before closing the sale that is the subject of the offer. The agent does not point out to the seller how this contingency could delay his closing. The seller accepts the offer, and then finds that the projected closing date is going to be missed by weeks, if not months.

■ Nondisclosure of Seller's Agent's Interest

In a transaction in which the licensee is an agent for the seller of real property, real estate law prohibits failing to disclose to the seller the nature and extent of any direct or indirect interest that the licensee expects to acquire as a result of the sale.

The licensee must disclose to the seller of a property that it is being purchased

- by a person related to the licensee by blood or marriage,
- by an entity in which the licensee has an ownership interest,
- by a person with whom the licensee occupies a special relationship, or
- where there is a reasonable probability that the licensee could be indirectly acquiring an interest in the property.

Example

A seller employed a licensed salesperson to sell his residence. The seller wanted $175,000 net for his property. The salesperson arranged an escrow in which the purchaser was his sister or her nominee without explaining this relationship to the seller. Escrow closed and the property was conveyed to the agent's wife.

The Department of Real Estate accused the agent of fraud and dishonest dealing and suspended his license for 90 days.

■ Nondisclosure of Agent's Interest (Buyer's Agent)

In a transaction in which the licensee is an agent for the buyer of real property, real estate law prohibits failing to disclose to the buyer the nature and extent of a licensee's direct or indirect ownership interest in such real property. The licensee must disclose to the buyer the direct or indirect ownership interest in the property by a person related to the licensee by blood or marriage, by an entity in which the licensee has an ownership interest, or by any other person with whom the licensee occupies a special relationship.

Example

A buyer's broker shows a client a home for sale that is owned by the broker's daughter. Even if the broker has no direct ownership interest, the regulation requires her to inform the buyer of the blood relationship to avoid any possibility or suspicion of a hidden conflict of interest.

■ Interest in Referrals

Real estate law prohibits failing to disclose to a principal for whom the licensee is acting as an agent any significant interest the licensee has in a particular entity when the licensee recommends the use of the services or products of such entity. Business and Professions Code §10177.4 sets out grounds for discipline of a real estate licensee who claims, demands, or receives a "kickback" for referral to any escrow agent, controlled escrow company, or underwritten title company.

Example

A licensee directs a buyer to apply for a loan with a particular lender whose loan officer is his broker's wife. She receives a commission for placement of the loan. The agent fails to disclose these facts to the borrower.

■ Unit 2 Review Quiz

1. Which action of the broker in the example on page 53 was a violation of the misrepresentation regulation?

   a. Advising the seller to list at the appraised value

   b. Advising the buyer to accept a lower price

   c. Leading the seller to believe in a falsely reduced market value while personally profiting from a resale transaction

   d. Consummating two transactions on the same property concurrently

2. It would be perfectly acceptable and ethical to obtain a written offer from a buyer for a property that is not listed for sale and then use that offer to obtain an exclusive listing to sell from the property owner.

   a. True

   b. False

3. A salesperson knows that the buyer's closing costs on a certain sale transaction are likely to be on the order of $2,000. The buyer wants to make an offer, but is concerned about coming up with enough cash for the down payment and the closing costs. To help the buyer decide to make the offer, the salesperson states that the seller usually pays all the closing costs. Comforted, the buyer makes the offer, only to learn about the $2,000 in closing costs that he is going to have to pay. What ethical or legal violation, if any, has the salesperson most likely committed?

   a. Underestimating closing costs to induce the buyer to make an offer

   b. Misrepresenting the buyer's ability to repay a note to the seller

   c. Misrepresenting to the seller the amount of the buyer's down payment

   d. Modifying the listing agreement without the buyer's authorization

4. A certain property is listed for sale at $350,500. A comparative market analysis indicates that its market value is about $300,000. The wiring and plumbing in the house are substandard and the lot, supposedly 150 feet deep, has not been surveyed. Which of the following representations could a listing agent make to a prospective buyer without a violation?

   a. He could tell a buyer that the lot was 150 feet deep.

   b. He could tell a lender that the house was worth $350,000.

   c. He could tell a buyer or lender that the house was in excellent condition.

   d. He could say that the house had "charm."

5. A salesperson tells a prospective renter that there will be no problem with operating the renter's mail order business from the rental house the salesperson is managing for the owner. The salesperson neglected to mention that local zoning prohibits at-home businesses in this neighborhood. If the renter signs the lease and then finds he cannot conduct his business as he intended, he may have the grounds for a complaint to the Department of Real Estate about the salesperson's behavior.

   a. True

   b. False

6. A salesperson is showing a country home to a prospective buyer. The buyer is attracted by the country setting and the fact that there are no strip malls anywhere within sight. The agent knows that the village has just granted a permit to a developer to put in a strip mall at a nearby intersection. The agent is under no obligation to give this information to the buyer.

   a. True

   b. False

Loan Transactions: Unlawful Conduct

The real estate law defines and prohibits unlawful acts and omissions when soliciting, negotiating, or arranging a loan secured by real property or the sale of a promissory note secured by real property.

The law prohibits acts and omissions in the following areas:

- Misrepresenting loan availability
- Misrepresenting borrower's qualifications
- Underestimating costs
- Misrepresenting priority of a lien
- "Free" services

- False information on loan payments
- Not accounting for advance fees
- Security property value or condition

■ Misrepresenting Loan Availability

Real estate law prohibits knowingly misrepresenting to a prospective borrower of a loan to be secured by real property or to an assignor/endorser of a promissory note secured by real property that there is an existing lender willing to make the loan or that there is a purchaser for the note, for the purpose of inducing the borrower or assignor/endorser to utilize the services of the licensee.

Example

A buyer completed an offer conditioned upon obtaining GI financing. Just prior to closing, the GI loan fell through. The broker then recommended that the buyer assume an existing first trust deed and a second trust deed that was due in full in six months. He stated that at the end of six months *he could arrange GI financing* because of the increased equity in the property.

Six months later, the agent was unable to obtain the promised GI financing. The owner was forced to sell the house to pay off the note secured by the second trust deed. The Department of Real Estate accused the broker of false and fraudulent misrepresentations and, after a hearing, revoked his license.

■ Misrepresenting Borrower's Qualifications

Real estate law prohibits:

- Knowingly making a false or misleading representation to a prospective lender or purchaser of a real estate loan about a borrower's ability to repay the loan in accordance with its terms and conditions
- Failing to disclose to a prospective lender or note purchaser information about the prospective borrower's financial qualifications as they were represented by the prospective borrower
- Failing to disclose information known to the broker relative to the ability of the borrower to meet potential or existing contractual obligations under the note or contract

Example

A broker is assisting her brother-in-law in finding and financing a first home. The broker knows that her brother-in-law has defaulted on his college loans, but "forgets" to tell the lender who is considering giving him a mortgage loan.

Financial Assistance Disclaimer

When a loan transaction involves a federally insured lender or federal loan program, the licensee should exercise extreme caution and supply a written disclaimer asserting the licensee's lack of knowledge about the accuracy, truth, or validity of the borrower's loan application or any supporting materials.

Penalty for Defrauding Loan Applications

The Financial Institutions Reform, Recovery, and Enforcement Act (FIRREA) provides for forfeiture to the United States of any real or personal property derived from proceeds traceable to "knowingly making any false statement . . . for the purpose of influencing in any way the action of . . . any institution the accounts of which are insured by the Federal Deposit Insurance Corporation (FDIC) upon any application for a loan."

■ Underestimating Costs

Real estate law prohibits knowingly underestimating the probable closing costs in a communication to a prospective borrower or lender of a real estate loan for the purpose of inducing the borrower or lender to enter into the loan transaction.

Example

A licensee encourages a homebuyer to accept a mortgage loan from ABC Loan Company by stating that ABC's loan origination fees and miscellaneous charges are "always" included in the points, when in fact these charges are extra and may amount to several hundred dollars.

■ Misrepresenting Priority of a Lien

Real estate law prohibits falsely representing, or representing without a reasonable basis to believe its truth, the priority of the lien against the real property securing the loan (i.e., a first, second, or third deed of trust).

Real estate licensees are expected to understand the significance of lien priority. The foreclosure of a prior lien "wipes out" the security of all junior liens. If there is no equity securing the junior lien, that lien is unsecured.

Example

A licensee is assisting a buyer in obtaining financing on a property. The agent finds a first lender willing to commit to a 70 percent loan-to-value loan. The buyer does not have the cash for a 30 percent down payment, so the broker persuades the seller to carry back a second trust deed for 25 percent of the price. The broker assures the seller that the loan is secure, since she could immediately foreclose on a default and get all her money back, just like the first trust deed lender. The broker is in potential violation of the regulation for representing the second lien as being equally safe and secure as the first lien—which it is not.

■ "Free" Services

Real estate law prohibits knowingly misrepresenting in any transaction that a specific service is free when the licensee knows or has a reasonable basis to know that it is covered by a fee to be charged as part of the transaction.

Example

Some buyers hired an agent to find them a home and assist in procuring financing. The agent found the home and arranged the loan, but failed to disclose that the buyers would be paying a $500 charge to the lender for the loan. The note signed by the buyers did not show the special charge. Instead, the closing statement showed a $500 charge added to the purchase price identified as a commission to the broker.

The DRE found that the agent had fraudulently concealed the fact that a $500 bonus to the lender was being charged as part of the transaction. The agent's license was subsequently revoked.

■ False Information on Loan Payments

Real estate law prohibits knowingly making a false or misleading representation about the amount and treatment of loan payments, including loan payoffs, and failing to account for the disposition of such payments to a lender or assignee/endorsee of a lender of a loan secured directly or collaterally by a lien on real property.

Example

A licensee is servicing a loan for a private lender. The licensee agrees that the borrower's monthly payment checks will be forwarded directly to the lender. The broker actually deposits the payments into a bank account he has set up for this purpose and then sends the lender checks drawn against that account.

■ Not Accounting for Advance Fees

Real estate law prohibits the failure to account to a borrower for the disposition of the "advance fee" when acting as a licensee in a transaction for the purpose of obtaining a loan and when in receipt of an advance fee from the borrower for this purpose.

Advanced Fee Documentation

Real estate law requires an accounting of advance fees collected and their disbursements. In the case of an advance fee for the arrangement of a loan secured by real property or a business opportunity, the accounting must contain a list of the names and addresses of the persons to whom information pertaining to the principal's loan requirements were submitted and the dates of the submittals.

■ Security Property Value or Condition

Real estate law prohibits knowingly making a false or misleading representation, or a representation without a reasonable basis for believing its truth, about the market value of the securing real property, the nature and/or condition of the interior or exterior features of the securing real property, its size, or the square footage of any improvements on the property, when soliciting a lender or negotiating a loan to be secured by a lien on real property.

Example

A borrower applies to a real estate broker for a second trust deed loan of $100,000 and assures the broker that the building has a value of at least $200,000. The broker fails to verify the value is correct and submits the loan application to a private lender and assures the lender that the building is indeed worth at least $200,000.

Responsibilities to Other Licensees

Duty of professionalism.   Real estate licensees are highly visible within their communities. Because of the acts of a few unscrupulous licensees, the public opinion of brokers and salespersons has suffered. If real estate licensees wish to be viewed as more than property merchants, they constantly must be aware not only of their own obligations, but also of the professional obligations of all licensees.

Keeping Up-to-Date

Continuing education is in place to keep licensees up-to-date on the myriad changes that occur in the business, including the areas of law, taxes, finance, disclosures, etc.

Don't Undermine Another Licensee

In general, criticizing fellow licensees has been strongly discouraged (even though it may be warranted). If asked, you should state facts and not opinions concerning other members of the profession. Making statements like "Why did you list with such a small office?" or "She does well considering her short time in the business," or, "Is that all they've done to market your property?" is both unprofessional and unethical.

Duty to Cooperate

The agent must cooperate with the other licensees wherever possible. This means to disseminate exclusive listings as quickly as possible. In cobroker arrangements, it is unethical to avoid answering reasonable requests for information in a timely manner or to withhold or unreasonably delay any offers received.

Hiring Practices

Ethical dealings with the people in your office must begin from the first day that new agents join the firm. It would be unethical for a broker to make statements regarding the unrealistic earnings/costs of belonging to a company. For example, implying that sales associates are earning more money than they really are and neglecting to be forthright about the expenses that will be incurred working in the business are considered unethical practices.

The broker should investigate the character of an employee or associate during the hiring process; the mere fact that the state has issued someone a license is no guarantee that the person is ethical. Remember, the broker is allowing a salesperson to represent the firm and its clients, as well as to act in a fiduciary manner. When a prospective salesperson has previously worked for other brokers, the hiring broker should do a reference check with the other broker(s) to determine the character of the salesperson.

Part-Time Sales Associates

Many people get started in real estate by working part-time. This term means different things to different people. It is critical to understand what the sales associate means by "part-time." A part-time salesperson's time may be greatly restricted, and this employee may have trouble following up on leads, previewing properties, or providing the service expected by the broker's clients/customers.

Avoiding Delays

If a broker is a member of a multiple listing service, it is unethical to intentionally take the maximum amount of time allowed for listing submissions when, in fact, the listing could have been submitted earlier with reasonable diligence. Such purposeful or negligent delays work to the detriment of the principal.

Interference with a Client

Without a prearranged procedure or express permission to do so, contacting another's client would be considered unethical behavior. Multiple listing services generally have rules governing when an agent may contact another broker's principal. The rules might require contacting a member of the association MLS committee prior to the licensee taking the liberty of contacting the owner.

Example

Realtor A, complainant, took a six-month listing on a property, entered it into MLS, put a sign on the lawn, and started marketing the property. Thirty days into the listing, the sellers called the complainant saying they wanted to go on vacation but did not want the house on the market while they were gone. The sellers asked the complainant to take the house off the market while they were gone. The complainant gave the sellers a conditional cancellation, removed the lockbox from the door, and removed the For Sale sign from the property.

After the sellers returned from vacation, realtor B, respondent, contacted the sellers during a routine prospecting session; the sellers said they were interested in selling. Two weeks later the respondent met with the sellers to list their house. Respondent learned the house had previously been listed and cancelled, but the sellers could not find the cancellation agreement. Since the sellers wanted the house back on the market, the respondent took the listing. Two days later when he was entering the listing in the MLS, he discovered the conditional cancellation, but proceeded to enter the listing into the MLS. Respondent contacted the complainant offering to work out a referral fee for the complainant. The offer was refused. Respondent cancelled his listing after an MLS representative informed him there were two listings on the property in question. Realtor B was found in violation of soliciting and taking a listing that was currently listed exclusively with another broker.

■ Unit 3 Review Quiz

1. A real estate licensee is permitted to encourage a homebuyer to make an offer to purchase by telling him that his broker will get him a loan through the local bank, even though the broker knows nothing about this buyer's qualifications.

   a. True

   b. False

2. A borrower applied for a purchase money loan from a federally insured lender to buy a personal residence. On his loan application, he stated that he earned $8,000 a month from a named employer. Relying on the borrower's financial statements, the lender approved the loan to the borrower, who purchased and occupied the subject dwelling.

   When the borrower defaulted on loan payments, the bank learned that the financial statements were false and reported the incident to the appropriate federal agencies. The real estate licensee who assisted the borrower in filling in the application could be in major trouble.

   a. True

   b. False

3. A mortgage broker began the practice of obtaining from customers the highest loan authorizations possible in order to receive higher commission amounts. He gave loan officers no instructions to advise prospective borrowers that the loan broker's compensation was limited by law on loans below a certain amount, but unlimited on loans that exceeded that amount. On loans over the regulated amount, the borrower would potentially end up paying considerably more for the loan. Disgruntled borrowers who were interviewed by investigators from the Department of Real Estate indicated that they had needed loan amounts that would have fallen within the limits of regulated loans but had authorized a greater loan at the suggesting of the loan officers.

   The loan broker in this instance is in violation of the regulation that prohibits underestimating closing costs to a borrower.

   a. True

   b. False

4. A broker made a practice of buying homes on his own account from highly motivated sellers who were willing to take back an unrecorded trust deed. After acquiring many properties in this way, the broker applied to institutional and other lenders for loans on these properties but failed to disclose the unrecorded trust deeds. After receiving loan funds, the broker intentionally defaulted on both the new senior liens given the lenders and the junior liens given the sellers. Which statement do you feel best describes the broker's actions and liabilities?

   a. He has obviously violated the regulation against misrepresenting lien priority.

   b. He has broken no laws or regulations.

   c. He has clearly broken the law but has not violated the regulation against misrepresenting lien priority.

   d. He has probably broken a law and violated the regulation against misrepresenting lien priority.

5. Which action would most likely violate the real estate law on loan transactions?

   a. Telling the prospective lender that the collateral property has been professionally remodeled when it hasn't been

   b. Telling the prospective borrower that there will be an expensive loan origination fee, knowing the borrower will not be able to afford it

   c. Refusing to give the prospective lender an opinion of market value for the collateral property

   d. Offering to provide a client with a "free" service

Suggestions for Professional Conduct

The real estate commissioner previously issued suggestions for professional conduct in sale, lease, and exchange transactions, and when negotiating or arranging real estate loans. The purpose of the suggestions was to encourage real estate licensees to maintain a high level of ethical standards and professionalism in their business practices.

These suggestions serve as a guide for positive professional conduct.

■ Conduct Areas Covered

The suggestions for professional conduct address the areas of:

- Advertising
- Arbitration
- Codes of ethics
- Communication
- Cooperation
- Discrimination
- Enforcement
- Expertise

- Knowledge
- Net proceeds
- Offers
- Refunding deposits
- Service
- Status reports
- Value opinions

■ Service

In the listing agreement, we promise to be diligent in finding a ready, willing, and able buyer. Diligence means presenting a marketing plan and carrying out that plan. Our word determines our integrity. It means showing up when you say you are going to be there or do something. If one is too busy (or disorganized), it means having to delegate activities to others so that you can keep your commitments.

■ Communication

Stay in close communication with clients, customers, borrowers, or lenders to ensure that questions are promptly answered. It is also important to maintain as much *personal* contact with customers/clients as possible, especially in the age of electronic communication. Questions need to be answered promptly, and all significant events or problems in a transaction need to be conveyed in a timely manner.

■ Enforcement

Cooperate with the California Department of Real Estate's enforcement of the real estate law and report evident violations to that department.

■ Advertising

Use care in the preparation of any advertisement to present an accurate picture or message to the reader, viewer, or listener.

■ Offers

Submit all written offers in a prompt and timely manner.

■ Knowledge

Keep informed and current on factors affecting the real estate market and the real estate loan market in which the licensee operates as an agent.

■ Cooperation

Make a full, open, and sincere effort to cooperate with other licensees, unless the principal has instructed the licensee to the contrary.

■ Arbitration

Attempt to settle disputes with other licensees through mediation or arbitration.

■ Expertise

Advertise or claim to be an expert in an area of specialization in real estate brokerage activity or real estate mortgage loan transactions (e.g., appraisal, property management, industrial siting, mortgage loan) *only* if special training, preparation, or experience supports the claim.

■ Discrimination Prohibited

Strive to provide equal opportunity for quality housing and quality mortgage loan services and a high level of service to all persons regardless of race, color, sex, religion, ancestry, physical handicap, marital status, or national origin. (Please see "Fair Housing" section at the end of this unit for more information.)

■ Value Opinions

Base opinions of value, whether for the purpose of advertising or promoting real estate brokerage business or mortgage loan business, upon documented objective data.

■ Refunding Deposits

Obtain written instructions from both parties to a transaction prior to disbursing a money deposit to a party.

■ Status Reports

Respond to reasonable inquiries of a principal as to the status or extent of efforts to negotiate the sale of an existing loan.

■ Net Proceeds

Respond to reasonable inquiries of a borrower regarding the net proceeds available from a loan arranged by the licensee.

■ Codes of Ethics

Make every attempt to comply with these suggestions for professional conduct and the code of professional conduct and the code of ethics of any organized real estate industry group or mortgage loan industry group of which the licensee is a member.

■ Fair Housing

In our increasingly diverse culture, another primary area of legal and ethical concern is treating all clients and customers in a nondiscriminatory manner. Both federal and state fair housing laws require that real estate licensees behave in a way that is color-blind. The most challenging situations occur when members of the public pose questions that either reveal a discriminatory point of view or suggest actions that would violate fair housing laws.

The following samples are intended to get licensees to think about appropriate (and ethical) ways of responding to these types of questions.

The exercises in this section will prepare you for situations in which a seller or buyer asks difficult questions, some of which are blatantly discriminatory and some of which are not.

For each of the following 12 situations, please do the following:

1. Read the question.
2. Formulate a response you believe would be appropriate.
3. Compare your response to the suggested answers that follow.

Situation 1:

You, the agent, have shown this house three times, once to a single Hispanic mother, once to two black males and once to a white elderly couple. It is the Hispanic single mother who has made this offer.

Seller question:

"Which buyer is this contract from?"

Suggested answer:

"This offer is from Ms. Juanita Rodriguez, the computer salesperson from Akron."

Important: NEVER answer, "The offer is from Ms. Juanita Rodriguez, the Latino woman."

Situation 2:

A black couple, one a computer programmer, the other a commodities trader, have made an offer on the house.

Seller question:

"What color are they?"

Suggested answer A:

"Before I try to answer your question, I need to know why you are asking it. As you know, our listing agreement provides that this property is offered without regard to color. If you intend to violate that agreement, I need to know up front so that we can save ourselves and each other a great deal of litigation and liability. I must protect myself and my company and, it is to be hoped, protect you."

Suggested answer B:

"Under the terms of our listing agreement and under the law, I am really reluctant to have you ask that question or to try to answer it. The color of the prospective buyer is really irrelevant, isn't it, to your desire to sell your property at the price and on the terms you consider fair? If you want one of those terms to be a buyer of a certain race, then frankly, we can't represent you and no other real estate broker in town can legally do so and keep her license."

Suggested answer C:

"Ms. Seller, I don't want to answer that question because whatever answer I give you will make the marketing of your property a great deal more complicated and costly for both of us. You and I are both obligated by law to offer your property without regard to color. If I answer your question, how are we ever going to be able to prove that we have fulfilled our legal obligation? No matter whether the buyer is black or white or some shade in between, we will have a lot of trouble proving that race was not a factor in your final decision to sell. And, really, it shouldn't be a factor if we can get you the price and terms you are looking for."

Situation 3:

Mr. and Mrs. Sanchez are Hispanic. They are financially qualified and have made an offer within $1,000 of the asking price. You have shown the house a number of times and feel that an offer from the O'Briens or possibly another white family may be forthcoming.

Seller question:

"Can I wait for Mr. and Mrs. O'Brien to make an offer? The Sanchez family isn't the type that I want to buy my home."

Suggested answer A:

"Ms. Seller, I don't understand why you don't believe Mr. and Mrs. Sanchez are the type you want to buy your home. They have made a good offer and are financially qualified. What type are you looking for?"

Important: If the response reveals that the seller is looking for a nonminority buyer, the broker should advise the seller of her legal and contractual obligation not to discriminate.

Suggested answer B:

"Mr. Seller, I certainly appreciate your desire to have the opportunity to consider all offers, so I will try to get an offer from the O'Briens immediately. But Ms. Sanchez's offer is a good one, and I would hate to see you lose out by delaying. Also, I really don't understand why you don't consider the Sanchezes to be the type to buy your home."

Important: Where the basis for deferring a decision is ambiguous but could be discriminatory, it is important that the broker attempt to remove the ambiguity by forcing the seller to articulate consent. If the concern is founded in bias, the broker is able to take action to remove or overcome the bias or repudiate any support for it. On the other hand, the concern may be the product of considerations or impressions that the broker can either clear up or explain in nondiscriminatory terms.

Situation 4:

Ms. Jones, the prospective buyer, is black. The house has been shown only three times in three months, and no one else seems interested.

Seller question:

"If I take my home off the market, how long do I have to wait before I can sell it again?"

Suggested answer A:

"Ms. Seller, you must understand that if you withdraw this property in order to avoid selling it to Ms. Jones (an African American), you risk serious legal liability and you may be unable to sell your property indefinitely. I strongly suggest you consult with your counsel before you take this action. As for me and my firm, I certainly cannot agree to the termination of our listing agreement for this reason."

Suggested answer B:

"Mr. Seller, I am very uncomfortable with your decision to withdraw your property from the market. I realize this is your decision, but I am concerned that it will appear to be merely an excuse not to sell to Ms. Jones (an African American). Perhaps you should rethink your decision."

Suggested answer C:

"Ms. Seller, I understand the reasons you feel you need to withdraw your property from the market. However, Ms. Jones may feel that they are merely excuses for not accepting her offer because she is black. I think it would be helpful to you and Ms. Jones, and it might avoid hard feelings, misunderstanding, and possible litigation, if I brought Ms. Jones by and let you explain your decision to her personally."

Important: Face-to-face meetings between seller and minority offeree have several values: First, the broker is relieved of the problem of articulating and explaining the reasons for the withdrawal. Second, the minority offeree is able to see that it is the seller and not the broker who has made the decision. Third, the mere bringing of seller and offeree together for a "final discussion" supports the objective role of the broker. Fourth, the prospect of confrontation may well discourage the seller whose reasons for withdrawing the property are not substantive or honest.

Situation 5:

This is a new listing in a community that is a white pocket in a racially mixed county.

Seller question:

"Are you aware that there is a bonus for selling my home to the 'right people'?"

Suggested answer A:

"I appreciate the offer of a bonus, but it would be both unethical and illegal for me to accept it when it is conditioned on the race, national origin, religion, handicap, familial status, or sex of the buyer I am able to bring you. Such an arrangement would subject each of us to very serious liability."

Suggested answer B:

"Your offer of a bonus for bringing you offers from the 'right' people is inconsistent with our agreement that I am to market your property without regard to race, religion, national origin, handicap, familial status, or sex of the home seeker. I must insist on holding you to your agreement."

Situation 6:

Seller is an elderly black college professor who lives in an upper class section of town. She is interested in seeing that the neighborhood stays integrated.

Seller question:

"Why must I sell my house to people I don't like, white or black? Why don't I have freedom of choice? What about my rights?"

Suggested answer A:

"Ms. Seller, I don't think it is appropriate for me to try to answer these questions for you. If you believe you have the right to discriminate on the basis of race, religion, national origin, handicap, familial status, or sex, I can only urge you to have a talk with your attorney."

Suggested answer B:

"From my standpoint, and that of my firm, we know we are prohibited by law and by our code of ethics from marketing property on a discriminatory basis. Moreover, it is difficult for us to understand how people can dislike a whole race, religion, nationality, sex, family status, or handicap. How can someone hate someone without knowing him or her? What does being a Jew have to do with being a good neighbor? What does being Italian have to do with the price you want for your property?"

Suggested answer C:

"We can do a good job of selling your property to a qualified buyer at the price and on the terms you specify. But, we cannot do that job unless we have your consent and support to market your property on a nondiscriminatory basis."

Situation 7:

This agent covers the entire south side of a major metropolitan area. The family is of Asian descent.

Buyer question:

"What is the racial composition of this neighborhood?"

Suggested answer A:

"We have a host of demographic information back at the office. You can review it when we return. It would not be wise for me to guess. If you'd like to research this matter, I have the telephone numbers for the city's planning department and the census bureau. They have additional information."

Situation 8:

The agent serves a wide, rural area.

Buyer question:

"I am black. Do you service any areas that I would feel at home in?"

Suggested answer A:

"We have access to houses for sale in many areas. If you can tell me some of the features you are looking for in either your house or neighborhood, I am sure I can help you out. Are there any particular villages or towns in which you would like to start your search? Most of the villages have houses in several price ranges, and the houses tend to vary quite a bit in style and age. Once I know what you're looking for, I'll be in a better position to let you know what is available that meets your criteria and to help you find the house in the area that you want."

Situation 9:

The agent serves an area with homes owned by a variety of races, ages, and religions. The agent's own children attend a school that is approximately 60 percent white, 20 percent black, 10 percent Hispanic, and a 10 percent mix of Native American and Asian.

Buyer question:

"Are the schools integrated?"

Suggested answer A:

"Our office does not maintain statistics regarding the racial makeup of the student body in the schools in our market area. If you would like such information, you should contact either the school itself or the school district's office. Those sources can also tell you which schools will be available to your children, class size, and basic curriculum, and provide the best answers to your questions. Also, you might want to check with some of your potential new neighbors about how they feel about the schools their children attend."

Suggested answer B:

"Mr. Buyer, the only school I'm really familiar with is the one my own children attend. Since I don't have personal experience with the others, I cannot give you the complete information you really want and need. Let me refer you to the school district office that can give you information about curriculum, class size, and the names of the schools that service the various neighborhoods in which you are interested."

Situation 10:

The prospective buyers are an elderly couple. The agent's area covers urban, suburban, and rural areas. There are pockets of high crime in the urban areas. The suburbs tend not to suffer from major crimes such as murder and armed theft, but they do have their share of purse-snatchings, shoplifting, and home break-ins. There are some adult communities in your area that have walls and security guards.

Buyers' question:

"Why don't you just pick out some nice properties in a safe area for us?"

Suggested answer A:

"We have many homes in our market area from which to choose. Perhaps we should inspect a few to see which ones best fit your needs."

Suggested answer B:

"Our office does not compile crime statistics. Let's go through our multiple listing of homes and select some that fit your requirements. While we're out inspecting homes, we can stop at the village police department if you would like to. Also, I can put you in touch with several security services who would undoubtedly be able to discuss your concerns in depth."

Situation 11:

You, the agent, live in a community similar to that of the home you are showing, but closer to the river. The home under consideration is in a relatively new subdivision. Your neighborhood is older, with larger homes and established trees. You have no children in school, as this buyer does.

Buyer question:

"Would you live here?"

Suggested answer A:

"Yes, I would. The area is well maintained and that particular house is very nicely located. It's very convenient to the commuter trains and shopping and the elementary school is only a few blocks away."

Suggested answer B:

"No, I wouldn't because the house is just too small for our teenager's activities."

Situation 12:

The client is a professional couple, second-generation Japanese Americans. They have two children.

Buyers' question:

"We're from out of town. Could you suggest some good areas?"

Suggested answer A:

"All of the areas in which we do business have many positive features. The communities, styles, and prices of housing do vary, however. What did you have in mind? Do you have any particular needs in a house?"

Suggested answer B:

"We're very positive about all the areas we service. Each community has its own particular charm, and, of course, no place is perfect. What size and style of home are you looking for? Are you familiar with any of the communities in which we have listings?"

■ Unit 4 Review Quiz

1. If you follow the former commissioner's suggestions for professional conduct, you will answer client questions and report transaction problems quickly.
   a. True
   b. False

2. The commissioner's suggestions for professional conduct advise agents to concentrate on marketing and leave the study of local market conditions to the experts.
   a. True
   b. False

3. It is not necessary to cooperate with other licensees in selling a listing unless your client instructs you to do so.
   a. True
   b. False

4. In advertising a property for sale, it is good professional conduct to be prepared to back up all claims and descriptions with data that has been documented by an objective source, such as an appraiser.
   a. True
   b. False

5. If you are arranging a loan for a homebuyer, good professional conduct requires that you answer the borrower's questions about the amount of the loan proceeds.
   a. True
   b. False

Unit 1 Review Answers

1. **a.** The Department of Real Estate licenses individuals to practice the profession of real estate and regulates their conduct. The laws and regulations contained in the California Business and Professions Code and the Code of Regulations apply to all brokers and salespersons licensed by the state of California.

2. **c.** Conflict of interest is one of the principal complaints leading to suspension or revocation of licenses. A conflict of interest occurs when an agent violates or evades the fiduciary relationship by such actions as fraudulent conduct, dual representation without disclosure, failure to disclose a financial interest in a transaction, undisclosed special relationships with buyer or seller, and commingling of funds.

3. **b.** Multiple listing service violations are one of the primary concerns of local associations, not the state association, which is more concerned with conflicts of interest, misrepresentation, and advertising.

Unit 2 Review Answers

1. **c.** The regulation prohibits deliberately misrepresenting market value to acquire an interest in the property for the licensee's own account.

2. **a.** The regulation prohibits representing to a seller in a listing negotiation that the licensee has a written offer to purchase when there is no such written offer. It does not prohibit obtaining a written offer prior to obtaining a listing.

3. **a.** Real estate law prohibits knowingly underestimating the probable closing costs in a communication to the prospective buyer of real property in order to induce that person to make an offer to purchase the property. The salesperson may or may not have been guilty of making misrepresentations to the seller.

4. **d.** The real estate law prohibits knowingly making a false or misleading representation of the nature or condition of the features of a property, but since a term such as "charm" is totally subjective and does not really describe any features, it would not be a violation.

5. **a.** The real estate law prohibits knowingly making a false or misleading representation to a prospective lessee that a property can be used for certain purposes in order to get the lessee to sign a lease.

6. **b.** The real estate law requires the licensee to disclose to a prospective purchaser facts the licensee knows and that the prospective purchaser cannot readily see when these facts might affect the desirability of the property to the purchaser.

Unit 3 Review Answers

1. **b.** The real estate law prohibits knowingly misrepresenting the existence or availability of a loan to a prospective borrower for the purpose of getting the borrower's business.

2. **a.** A real estate licensee who helped this buyer apply for the loan could have been exposed to action for both civil and criminal acts. A federal court seized the property in this case.

3. **a.** The regulation prohibits underestimating the probable closing costs to induce the borrower into the loan transaction. The Department of Real Estate found that the loan broker's conduct violated various provisions within the Business and Professions Code and imposed discipline ranging from suspensions to revocations.

4. **c.** When the lenders and sellers complained, the broker was convicted of criminal fraud and grand theft and sentenced to prison. As for the real estate law, it did not strictly apply. However, California law provides that a real estate licensee found guilty of a crime involving moral turpitude might be subject to suspension or revocation of the real estate license. The broker in this case could lose his real estate license as well as serve a prison term.

5. **a.** The regulation prohibits knowingly making a false representation to a prospective lender about the nature and/or condition of the interior or exterior features of the securing real property.

Unit 4 Review Answers

1. **a.** The commissioner's suggestions for professional conduct advise staying in close communication with clients, customers, borrowers, and lenders.

2. **b.** The commissioner's suggestions advise agents keep informed and current on factors affecting their local real estate markets and the real estate loan markets.

3. **b.** The commissioner's suggestion is to cooperate unless instructed not to do so. In this way, you can provide better service for your client.

4. **a.** The commissioner's suggestions advise licensees to base all opinions of value, including those promoted in advertising, on documented objective data.

5. **a.** The commissioner's suggestions advise the licensee to respond to a borrower's reasonable inquiries regarding the net proceeds of a loan the licensee is arranging.

Course 3: Fair Housing Laws

Introduction to Fair Housing Laws

Many state and federal laws, Supreme Court decisions, executive orders, and regulations make it unlawful for owners, agents, and business establishments to discriminate on the basis of race, color, sex, sexual preference, religion, ancestry, disability, marital status, familial status, age, or national origin.

When real estate licensees perform any licensed activities, it is both required and prudent for them to avoid engaging in any discriminatory activities. Violators face not only civil litigation for damages to injured persons, but may also face disciplinary action by the Department of Real Estate.

Fair Housing Legislation and Regulation

Federal and state laws, regulations, and court decisions since the Civil Rights Act of 1866 have collectively banned the practice of discrimination in housing against American citizens based on race, color, religion, national origin, gender, disability, or familial status.

This unit and the one following ("Discriminatory Acts") review the central thrusts of fair housing legislation and regulations: which people they affect, which ones they protect, and what the law prohibits.

The principal federal acts, regulations, and decisions are:

- Civil Rights Act of 1866
- *Shelley v. Kraemer*
- Federal Fair Housing Act (Civil Rights Act of 1968)
- *Jones v. Mayer*
- 1988 Amendments to the Federal Fair Housing Act

The landmark California laws and regulations are:

- California Civil Code Section 53
- California Civil Code §§51–52 (Unruh Civil Rights Act)
- California Fair Employment and Housing Act (Rumford Act)
- Department of Real Estate Commissioner's Regulations §§2780–2782

Federal Fair Housing Law

Civil Rights Act of 1866

The Civil Rights Act was passed by Congress over the veto of President Andrew Johnson. The act declared that all persons born in the United States were now citizens, without regard to race, color, or previous condition. As citizens they could make and enforce contracts, sue and be sued, give evidence in court, and inherit, purchase, lease, sell, hold, and convey real and personal property. Persons who denied these rights to former slaves were guilty of a misdemeanor and upon conviction faced a fine not exceeding $1,000 or imprisonment not exceeding one year, or both. The activities of organizations such as the Ku Klux Klan undermined the workings of this act and it failed to guarantee the civil rights of African Americans. The act did not extinguish the practice of private discrimination through restrictive covenants.

Example

A neighborhood might disallow ownership and residency of any property within it by a person of a specific race or color, as provided for in the deed of conveyance. Since "valid" deed restrictions were enforceable, a group of persons could be barred from ownership within that neighborhood.

Shelley v. Kraemer

In 1948, the U.S. Supreme Court ruled in *Shelley v. Kraemer* that it was unconstitutional to use deed restrictions to exclude individuals from housing because of race, color, religion, origin, or ancestry. The ruling was based upon the Fourteenth Amendment to the U.S. Constitution (effective 1868), granting equal protection of the law to all individuals.

Restrictive covenants were thereby unenforceable. However, the ruling did not prohibit the making of private agreements.

Federal Fair Housing Act (Civil Rights Act of 1968)

The cornerstone of federal fair housing law is Title VIII of the Civil Rights Act of 1968. This law bars discrimination in the sale, rental, or financing of any dwelling, or land to be used for a dwelling, based on race, color, religion, national origin, sex, handicap, or familial status.

- To "bar all racial discrimination, private as well as public and sophisticated as well as obvious"
- Discrimination in sale, rental, financing, or provision of services
- Indicating discriminatory preference in advertising
- Channeling, steering, blockbusting, and panic selling
- Criminal penalties for using force or threat of force
- Limited exemption for noncommercial dwelling units of private clubs and religious organizations

Jones v. Mayer

In 1968, the Supreme Court in *Jones v. Mayer* prohibited private as well as public discrimination in the exercise of citizens' property rights with no exemptions. Since the ruling eliminated all "exemptions" from discrimination, it reflectively rendered restrictive covenants illegal as well as unenforceable.

The Supreme Court stated: "It appears to have been the express intent of Congress, in plain and unambiguous language and terms to grant to all citizens, without regard to race or color, 'the same right' to purchase and lease property 'as is enjoyed by white citizens.' On its face, par. 1982 appears to prohibit all discrimination against Negroes in the sale or rental of property, whether it involves discrimination by private owners or public authorities, and what it means is what it says."

1988 Amendments to the Federal Fair Housing Act

The federal Fair Housing Act of 1988 amended the 1968 act to include two new protected classes: "familial status" and "handicap" (disability). After March 12, 1989, it became illegal to refuse to rent or sell to people for the reason that they have children or a physical or mental disability, to refuse to deal with them, or to treat them in any different fashion.

■ Disability does not include drug addiction; protection is not intended to cause landlords additional liability or expense, but must make "reasonable accommodations."

■ Familial status protects families with children, exemption for senior housing with strict age limits, or "significant facilities and services" for seniors.

■ Pattern or practice of certain acts constitutes discrimination even without showing of intent (e.g., differential treatment, procedural roadblocks, and misrepresentation).

■ Professional real estate organizations and services (e.g., Boards, MLS) must not discriminate in membership.

■ Enforcement by complaint to HUD, the attorney general, or private litigation.

■ California Fair Housing Legislation and Regulation

California Civil Code Section 53

Enacted in 1961, Civil Code Section 53 took measures against restrictive covenants. It provides that "any provision in any deed of real property . . . which purports to restrict the right of any persons to sell, lease, rent, use, or occupy the property to persons of a particular racial, national, or ethnic group, by providing for payment of a penalty, forfeiture, reverter, or otherwise, is void."

The Unruh Civil Rights Act (California Civil Code §§51–52)

The Unruh Civil Rights Act prohibits all arbitrary discrimination by business establishments, including real estate offices, property management companies, landlords, and homeowners' associations. It protects essentially the same classes as the federal Fair Housing Act. Exemptions are very limited.

■ Legislature added other protected classes: sex, age, disability, and sexual orientation.

■ "Business" includes selling and renting property, even a single building.

■ Extends to all arbitrary discrimination, specifically families with children.

■ Age restrictions are permitted for senior housing and developments providing special services.

■ Prohibits violence or threat of violence based on discriminatory categories

■ Remedies include injunctive relief, civil damages, and possible criminal penalties.

Rumford Act (California Fair Employment and Housing Act)

The Rumford Act, or the California Fair Employment and Housing Act, prohibits discrimination based on age, sex, race, color, religion, ancestry, national origin, disability, and/or familial status in the areas of employment and housing. The law prohibits discrimination in the sale, rental, lease, and/or financing of virtually all types of housing, with the exception of single-family houses with no more than one roomer or boarder.

- Employer is responsible for discriminatory acts of employees or agents.
- Administered by Department of Fair Employment and Housing.
- Remedies include making subject property available, providing another property, or actual and punitive damages.

Department of Real Estate Commissioner's Regulations §§2780–2782

The aim of the DRE in its regulations is "to achieve a 'color-blind' real estate industry that can help attain peaceful equal opportunity and fair housing for society." To achieve this, "the primary attitude of a licensee should be one which is color-blind and absolutely without bias."

Commissioner's Regulations Section 2780 defines discriminatory conduct in the sale, rental, or financing of real property as a basis for disciplinary action against licensees if based upon "race, color, sex, religion, ancestry, physical handicap, marital status, or national origin." It also prohibits panic selling and affirms the broker's duty to supervise.

- Broker is responsible for adherence to fair housing laws within the firm.
- Section 2782 establishes broker's duty to supervise.
- Licensee may decline to serve a disable person if beyond licensee's skills.

■ Applicability of Fair Housing Laws

Affected Properties

Title VIII of the Civil Rights Act of 1968, the federal Fair Housing Act, applies to any dwelling or land intended to be used for a dwelling or housing project, and applies "as thoroughly and as widely as is permissible under the broadest applicable reading of the Constitution."

According to California's Rumford Act, housing means any building, structure, or portion thereof, occupied or intended for occupancy as a residence by one or more families, and any vacant land offered for sale or lease for residential construction.

Section 2780 of the Department of Real Estate regulations applies to all real properties. A residential property development company, therefore, could not discriminate in selling or leasing an apartment building it constructed. Real estate licensees would be prohibited from discriminating regardless of whether the property was an apartment building, a theater, or an office complex.

Affected Parties

The Rumford Act prohibits discrimination by property "owners." A property owner includes a lessee, sublessee, assignee, managing agent, real estate broker or salesperson, or any person having any legal or equitable right of ownership or possession or right to rent or lease housing accommodations, including the state and any of its political subdivisions and any agency thereof.

The Unruh Act prohibits all arbitrary discrimination by "business establishments." Court decisions have established that business establishments include all professional services of real estate licensees, as well as the "business" of renting or selling property, even if that is not how the owner earns a living.

The Department of Real Estate's antidiscrimination regulations apply to all licensees.

Affected Activities

The Rumford Act applies to all residential real estate–related transactions, including:

- Sale, rental, or lease of property
- Making or purchasing of loans secured by real estate
- Providing financial services for the purpose of purchasing, constructing, improving, repairing, or maintaining a dwelling
- Selling, brokering, or appraising property

The Department of Real Estate's Section 2780 applies to the full range of real estate services offered by licensees, notably the sale, rental, or financing of real property.

Protected Classes

The general import of fair housing law is to include all citizens under its umbrella of protection against discrimination. The law, however, also identifies specific "protected classes," presumably to dispel any misunderstanding about the law's applicability.

Protected Classes, by Act

Federal Fair Housing Act (as amended): race, color, religion, national origin, sex (gender), handicap (disability), or familial status.

Unruh Civil Rights Act: race, color, religion, ancestry or national origin, sex, age, disability, and sexual orientation.

Rumford Act: race, religious creed, color, national origin, ancestry, physical disability, mental disability, medical condition, marital status, sex, and age.

Refinements of Protected Classes

The federal **Fair Housing Act of 1988:** This act amended the 1968 Fair Housing Act to include two new protected classes: "familial status" and "handicap" (disability). After March 12, 1989, it is illegal to refuse to rent to, sell to, or deal with people because they have children or a physical or mental disability, or to provide them with differential treatment. It is no longer legal to have buildings, sections of buildings, or floors of buildings designated as "all-adult." In such cases, it would be illegal to exclude a married couple with children under 18 years of age.

The definition of disability includes alcoholism, but the law does not give special protection to current drug addicts or persons who have been convicted of a drug-related felony. The law does not intend for owners to incur any greater liability in renting to persons in a protected class than they would in renting to anyone else. Thus, a landlord could refuse to rent to a known cocaine addict and not be liable for a fair housing violation.

Protected Classes Under Unruh: The original Unruh Act provided that all persons, regardless of "race, color, religion, ancestry, or national origin are entitled to the full and equal accommodations, advantages, facilities, privileges, or services in all business establishments of every kind whatsoever." Subsequent legislation added specific protected categories of sex (1974), age (1984), disability, and sexual orientation. The Unruh Act has been interpreted by courts to prohibit arbitrary discrimination of all types, not just those specifically listed in the act (e.g., against families with children or based on sexual preference).

The Unruh Act originally made no reference to age as a discriminatory category. In 1982 and 1983, the California Supreme Court held that the intent of the Unruh Act includes discriminatory prohibitions based upon age. Further, it held that even a single-family residence rental constitutes a business, and that it is illegal to exclude a prospective tenant based upon age. Refusal to rent to families with children was effectively prohibited.

■ Exemptions and Exceptions

Individual Owner Exception

Individual owners of not more than three houses are exempt from federal fair housing law as long as the sale or rental is accomplished without a real estate broker and without discriminatory advertising.

Example

An accountant could legally refuse to sell her principal residence to a Hispanic buyer on a for-sale-by-owner basis. The accountant, however, could not legally do so if she owned three other houses. Her advertising, finally, could not make mention of her discriminatory preference.

Under the Rumford Act, "discrimination" does not include refusal to rent or lease a portion of an owner-occupied single-family house to one individual roomer or boarder living within the household, provided the owner does not issue any discriminatory notices, statements, or advertisements.

Senior Housing Exemption

There are two senior housing communities that are exempt from federal fair housing:

- Those that show an intention to house older people and in which all the residents are or will be age 62 or older
- Those that show an intention to house older people and in which at least 80 percent of the units have or will have one person age 55 or older, and that provide "significant facilities and services" for the elderly

Similarly, the Unruh Act allows age restrictions on housing for seniors who need special environments and services. Also, specific "senior citizen housing developments" may be exempt. Still other exemptions may apply to a spouse, cohabitant, or person providing primary physical or economic support to the senior ("qualified permanent resident").

■ Enforcement and Penalties

Federal Fair Housing Law Enforcement

Persons claiming violations of federal fair housing laws must file a complaint with the Secretary of Housing and Urban Development (HUD) within one year. Administrative law judges at HUD decide fair housing cases, unless one of the parties demands a jury trial. Judges can award damages, injunctive relief, and attorney's fees, as well as impose fines. The Department of Justice prosecutes cases where defendants opt for court hearings. Punitive damages and jail sentences are possible in addition to fines.

California Fair Housing Law Enforcement

The Department of Fair Employment and Housing (DFEH) receives, investigates, and conciliates complaints under both the Rumford Act and the Unruh Act. It may provide local assistance in resolving disputes "when, in its judgment, peaceful relations among the citizens of the community involved are threatened."

Housing complaints must be filed with the Fair Employment and Housing Commission (FEHC) within 60 days of the alleged violation. The FEHC may investigate and render an administrative opinion. The complainant may also file in court.

Enforcement and Penalties

If the commission or the court affirms the complaint, several alternative remedies are available. The commission or court may:

- Order the owner to sell or rent the property to the person, if it is still available, or sell or rent other property if the person so desires
- Award actual and punitive damages if the foregoing remedy is not possible

---

Example

Assume a complainant was discriminated against in the rental of an apartment, and the commission confirmed the violation in its investigation. If the landlord rented the subject apartment to another party, and there were no other vacancies in the complex, the landlord could be ordered to pay damages to the complainant.

Violation of the Department of Real Estate Regulations

Discriminatory conduct by licensees violates DRE regulations and is grounds for disciplinary action, including possible license suspension or revocation. In addition, discrimination by a licensee is a violation of the Business and Professions Code.

Broker's Duty to Supervise

Section 2725 establishes the broker's duty to supervise: "A broker shall exercise reasonable supervision over the activities of his or her salespersons. Reasonable supervision includes . . . (f)amiliarizing salespersons with the requirements of federal and state laws relating to the prohibition of discrimination."

■ Unit 2 Review Quiz

1. The Civil Rights Act of 1866 effectively put an end to housing discrimination between whites and blacks in America.
   a. True
   b. False

2. The purpose of the Rumford Act is to prohibit discrimination in the area of employment as well as housing.
   a. True
   b. False

3. Real estate professionals are prohibited from discriminating in the sale of which of the following properties?
   a. One- to four-unit residential properties
   b. Residential properties, not including the professional's own home
   c. All residential properties
   d. All properties

4. A landlord refused to rent to Adam Tufluck. Adam was middle-aged, single, employed, able, and of sound mind. He was also the only applicant with a job. When Adam asked the landlord what the problem was, the landlord said he didn't "like" Adam, and that he didn't have to rent to him since he didn't belong to one of those "protected classes." Which of the following best applies?
   a. Adam has been discriminated against but has no legal recourse.
   b. Adam has been discriminated against but has no legal recourse until he joins a protected class.
   c. Adam may legitimately pursue a discrimination complaint against the landlord.
   d. The landlord was right and acted legally.

5. An individual Jewish homeowner places an ad through a real estate periodical to rent her home. The ad states that Jewish couples with no kids and no pets are preferred. Since the owner owns only one home, she has not violated any laws.
   a. True
   b. False

6. A discrimination complaint is better handled under state fair housing law than federal, since the complainant may not seek redress in court if HUD fails to find merit in the complaint.
   a. True
   b. False

Discriminatory Acts

It is unlawful to discriminate in providing real estate services to the public. Court cases have established that the Fair Housing Act prohibits any *pattern or practice* of discrimination involving certain types of actions, *even without showing of intent.* These groups of actions may be categorized as:

- Failure, avoidance, or refusal to render services
- Encouraging discrimination
- Discriminatory misrepresentation
- Misrepresenting property availability
- Discriminatory advertising
- Creating barriers and obstructions to the transaction
- Unequal or inconsistent services
- Discriminatory terms and conditions of sale
- Discriminatory management practices
- Inconsistent or burdensome application procedures
- Zoning
- Steering
- Blockbusting and panic selling
- Use of force, threats, and retaliation
- Restrictive covenants

■ Failure, Avoidance, or Refusal to Render Services

- Refusing to negotiate for or to sell, rent, or lease housing accommodations to any person
- Refusing to sell or rent after a bona fide offer has been made
- Failing to volunteer information about real property
- Failing to cooperate with another licensee in negotiating the sale, rental, or financing of real property
- Soliciting sales, rentals, or listings of real estate from any person but not from another person within the same area
- Refusing to accept a rental or sale listing based on characteristics of the owner or any occupants in the area

- Entering into an agreement, or carrying out instructions, not to show, lease, sell, or finance property
- Discriminating against owners or occupants of real property because of their visitors

Encouraging Discrimination

- Making any effort to encourage discrimination against persons in the showing, sale, lease, or financing of real property
- Committing any act that in context expresses or implies a limitation, preference, or discrimination

  For instance, assume an agent has a listing in an all-white neighborhood. An associate salesperson tells the agent he intends to show the house to a nonwhite prospect. The listing agent shrugs his shoulders and asks who else the associate has for potential showings, saying, "Are you familiar with that neighborhood?"

- Assisting any person when there are reasonable grounds to believe that the person intends to discriminate

Discriminatory Misrepresentation

- Making false statements or misrepresentations motivated by racial discrimination with the result that someone is unable to purchase or rent a dwelling or lot
- Quoting property values based on characteristics of residents in the area

Misrepresenting Property Availability

- Making false representations as to the availability of a dwelling unit
- Representing that a housing accommodation is not available for inspection, sale, or rental when in fact it is so available; any other denial or withholding of housing accommodations
- Discriminating with respect to the future availability of real property
- Placement of "sold" or "rented" signs in front of houses in a predominantly white neighborhood to discourage persons of other races from inquiring

Discriminatory Advertising

- Indicating any preference in advertising or statements, oral or written

  Consider the following common advertising phrases:

  > "perfect for the newlywed"
  > "ideal bachelor's pad"
  > "first-time buyer special"
  > "excellent for retirement"

  Are these phrases discriminatory? You be the judge.

- Publishing discriminatory advertising by restricting or enhancing the exposure or appeal to persons of a particular category

■ Creating Barriers and Obstructions to the Transaction

- Imposing artificial, arbitrary, and unnecessary barriers to the transaction process based on racial or other impermissible classification
- Making any effort to obstruct, retard, or discourage the purchase, lease, or financing of real property

---

Example

Agent Roy knows mortgage brokers in town with reputations for being very slow, or alternately, very fast. Would it be a coincidence if Roy were found to have referred all black prospects to the slowest mortgage broker and all white prospects to the most expeditious?

■ Unequal or Inconsistent Services

- Offering different levels and standards of service to different individuals
- Referring prospects to other licensees
- Using codes to identify minority prospects
- Assigning licensees based upon any discriminatory category
- Charging or quoting different prices to different individuals
- Discriminating against any person in making any determination of financial ability
- Limiting opportunity for any person to secure real property through a multiple listing or other real estate service

Providing unequal or inconsistent service commonly occurs in the context of screening prospects before showing them listings. The problem arises when agents vary their questioning and qualifying according to the race or nationality of the prospect instead of the circumstances of purchasing preference or capability. When agent Amy typically spends two hours with Hispanic prospects before showings and 15 minutes with white prospects, she could indeed have a problem on her hands based on providing unequal service.

Materiality of Race, Color, and Creed in Rendering Services

The attorney general of California has rendered an official opinion that mentioning a person's race, color, or creed is not a "material fact" in the sale or rental of property. Therefore, a broker or manager should not inquire as to the race, color, or religion of a prospective buyer or renter, and should not disclose such information to the owner if asked to do so.

■ Discriminatory Terms and Conditions of Sale

- Cancellation or termination of a sale or rental agreement based on race, religion, etc.
- Discriminating against any person in the terms and conditions of sale or rental of real property

---

Example

An agent suggests a 30-day financing contingency for a marginally qualified minority buyer. What if, upon investigation of the agent's previous contracts, it is found that his typical financing contingency is 60 days? Why only 30 days for the minority buyer?

- Charging excessive buyer's closing costs or other financing charges

Discriminatory Management Practices

- Discriminating in providing management services
- Overt rejection of rental applicants based on race
- Owner's failure to instruct and control management employees whose conduct produces discriminatory results
- Creation of unusual or impossible burdens of performance in a manner that produces discriminatory results

Inconsistent or Burdensome Application Procedures

- Arbitrary and uncontrolled rental procedures that produce discriminatory results
- Imposition of more burdensome application procedures, delaying tactics, or other forms of discouragement
- Processing applications more slowly or otherwise than normal to delay, hinder, or avoid the sale, rental, or financing of real property

Zoning

- Provision of segregated or separated housing accommodations

A particular zoning is illegal when there is no factual basis for its existence, and it is shown to have a discriminatory effect.

Steering

- Channeling or steering any person toward or away from a neighborhood based on their race, color, religions, creed, or national ancestry
- Making any effort to prevent any person from acquiring real property due to alleged community opposition

Blockbusting and Panic Selling

- Attempting to persuade owners to sell or rent by making representations about the entry into the neighborhood of certain classes of people
- Preying upon fears of property owners in racially transitional areas and areas being desegregated to create panic selling that results in community instability

Blockbusting and panic selling need not be blatant or obvious. Consider an agent who tells homeowners in the Rosewood neighborhood that the city planning commission is scheduling a vote on demolishing a low-income housing project in the worst crime area in the city and that the demolition might disperse existing tenants into Rosewood. "But the vote might go through anyway," he says.

California DRE Definition of Blockbusting

Brokers are prohibited from "committing the illegal act in inducing the sale, lease, or listing of residential property by stating or implying that loss of value, increase of crime, or decline in quality of schools will result if persons of a certain race, religion, ancestry, or national origin enter the neighborhood."

Definition of Panic Selling—Section 2781

"Prohibited discriminatory conduct includes, but is not limited to, soliciting sales or rental listings, making written or oral statements creating fear or alarm, transmitting written or oral warnings or threats, or acting in any other manner so as to induce or attempt to induce the sale or lease of real property through any representation, express or implied, regarding the present or prospective entry of one or more persons of another race, color, sex, religion, ancestry, marital status, or national origin into any area or neighborhood."

■ Use of Force, Threats, or Retaliation

- Threatening or forcing prospective buyers or renters by lawsuit or litigation into abandoning purchase or rental
- Making any effort to coerce, intimidate, threaten, or interfere with any person's right to move from or not move into a particular area
- Punishing licensees for their refusal to discriminate
- Taking retaliatory action because a person filed a fair housing complaint or undertook other lawful efforts to promote fair housing

Federal Fair Housing Penalties

It is illegal to use force or the threat of force to intimidate, interfere with, or retaliate for a person's attempt to participate in or finance a real estate transaction. Penalty may be imprisonment (10 years to life) and up to $10,000 fine, if the victim suffers bodily injury or dies.

■ Restrictive Covenants

Under the Unruh Act, every provision in a written instrument prohibiting or restricting the conveyance, encumbrance, leasing, or mortgaging of real property based on any of the prohibited discriminatory categories is void. As a result, where discriminatory covenants were once *enforceable*, then ruled *unenforceable*, they are now completely *illegal*.

■ Unit 3 Review Quiz

1. An agent refuses to present a 90 percent offer from a nonwhite couple, saying he has instructions from the owner that all reviewable offers must be at least 95 percent of the listed price. Three days later, the agent presents an 85 percent offer from a white family, and the owner accepts. The *agent's* actions have likely violated fair housing laws.

   a. True
   b. False

2. Lee Chen, a residential developer, has just constructed a condominium building in his Asian neighborhood to address the housing shortage for incoming relatives and friends from Taiwan. He intends to market the properties specifically to those groups. Lee's son, Michael, is a new licensee and eager to help with the listing and selling. What is the best advice to Michael to avoid discrimination liability?

   a. Restrict advertising to Taiwan to avoid U.S. fair housing laws
   b. Elicit cobrokerage participation to avoid exclusive representation
   c. Show the listing to all prospective buyers
   d. Avoid taking his father's listing

3. An agent's ad for a home listing reads:

   "Had it with downtown crime? Tired of kids screaming next door? Want to be where the preferred transportation is a golf cart, and the talk of the neighborhood is about grandchildren? Don't miss this golden opportunity of the Ages!"

   What, if anything, is wrong with this ad?

   a. It discriminates against the downtown location of the property.
   b. It discriminates against a specific race.
   c. It discriminates against people who are not elderly.
   d. There is nothing wrong with the ad.

4. In May, an agent tells a Caucasian buyer that she qualifies for a specific house. In November, the same agent tells a Hispanic buyer, with the same cash and income, that he does not qualify for the same house at the same price. This is a clear instance of discrimination in determining financial ability.

   a. True
   b. False

5. A property manager was tired of evicting marginally qualified tenants who subsequently could not make rent payments. To improve matters, he instructed his leasing employees to obtain recommendations from previous landlords on all black and Hispanic applicants who were not employed, or who had only been employed for less than a year. In this instance, the manager

   a. is guilty of unfair employment practices.
   b. is guilty of causing burdensome application procedures.
   c. has instituted discriminatory rental procedures.
   d. has not violated fair housing law since it is legal to screen out unqualified tenants.

6. A Mexican person asks an agent which neighborhoods in the city have the best appreciation. The agent responds that the best Hispanic neighborhood is the Alta Vista area, which is appreciating because of the good reputation of the schools. The agent then informs the prospect that there are other fine neighborhoods, but they are not "on top of the list." "I have to mention these so people won't think I'm steering you." But he has in fact steered the prospect.

   a. True
   b. False

7. In a previous scenario, management employees were instructed to obtain leasing recommendations for any black or Hispanic applicant with a marginal employment status. One of the rental agents, however, was Hispanic and didn't like the policy. Ignoring it, she leased an apartment to a Hispanic person without calling previous landlords. Six months later, the tenant defaulted and was evicted. The irritated manager placed a letter of reprimand in the agent's personnel file, and subsequently fired her after things had quieted down somewhat. In this case,

   a. fair employment laws protect the manager, since a letter of reprimand preceded the termination.
   b. the agent has little recourse, since she in fact violated management policy.
   c. the manager can justify the termination, since the agent discriminated against other minorities by renting to a Hispanic.
   d. the manager is liable for punishing an agent's refusal to discriminate.

Fair Housing in Advertising: HUD Regulations

Published Real Estate Advertising

HUD regulations require that published real estate advertising must include an Equal Housing Opportunity logo and a prescribed fair housing statement and slogan. In addition, publishers must make a separate equal opportunity statement and comply with guidelines for use of human models in display advertising.

Logo, Statement, and Slogan

Depending on the size of an advertisement, the equal housing logo must be displayed from one-half inch to two inches square, the equal housing statement given 3 to 5 percent of the space in the ad, or the slogan "Equal Housing Opportunity" used.

Publishers' Notice

The publisher of a real estate advertising section must introduce the section with a notice that states: "A real estate advertised herein is subject to the Federal Fair Housing Act." The notice may also cite any local fair housing or human rights ordinances prohibiting housing discrimination.

Notice to Employees and Clients

Publishers of advertising and firms engaged in the sale, rental, or financing of real estate must provide copies of their nondiscrimination policy to employees. Publishers and advertising agencies must post their nondiscrimination policy in a place conspicuous to clients.

■ Use of Human Models

If models are used in a display, they must "be clearly definable as reasonably representing majority and minority groups in the metropolitan area, both sexes, and, when appropriate, families with children," and "portray persons in an equal social setting" indicating that the housing is open to all "and is not for the exclusive use of one such group."

■ Fair Housing Poster

HUD requires that all persons and entities subject to the Fair Housing Act display a prescribed fair housing poster "so as to be readily apparent to all persons seeking housing accommodations or seeking to engage in residential real estate–related transactions or brokerage services."

Displaying the Fair Housing Poster

A real estate broker, agent, salesperson, or "person in the business of selling or renting dwellings" must display the poster at any place of business where dwellings are offered for sale or rental. For new homes covered by the act, the poster must be on display throughout the period of construction and sale or rental.

Enforcement

Failure to display the fair housing poster is deemed prima facie evidence of a discriminatory housing practice in the event that a person claiming to have been injured by a discriminatory housing practice files a complaint with HUD.

Example

Assume a broker does not display the fair housing poster. Then, on a particular occasion, he refuses to show a property, claiming it is already under contract. If the property is in fact available and a complaint is filed, the broker's refusal to display the poster is further evidence that the infraction in fact occurred.

■ Lenders

Savings associations are prohibited from using any advertising that "implies or suggests a policy of discrimination or exclusion," and advertisements other than for savings must include the logo:

EQUAL HOUSING
OPPORTUNITY

Savings associations must post at least one copy of a prescribed fair lending poster in the lobby "in a prominent place or places readily apparent to all persons seeking loans." A Spanish language version is recommended in areas with substantial Spanish-speaking population.

■ Unit 4 Review Quiz

1. The purpose of displaying the fair housing poster is to assure all buyer prospects that they will receive a fair deal when they purchase a home, regardless of from whom they purchase the home.

   a. True

   b. False

Voluntary Fair Practice: VAMA (Discontinued)

In 1975, the Department of Housing and Urban Development (HUD) and the National Association of Realtors® (NAR) coauthored the Voluntary Affirmative Marketing Agreement to promote affirmative fair housing practices. The VAMA was developed to educate Realtor® members on fair housing laws and to provide a set of specific fair housing procedures for members to use. However, in a recent review of the program, HUD officials and NAR members determined that too much emphasis had been placed on collecting VAMA signatures, and too little time was spent developing fair housing programs. Further, Realtors® often found VAMA regulations burdensome and process-oriented.

Consequently, HUD and NAR entered into discussions for the implementation of a new approach in fair housing cooperation. A new Fair Housing Partnership Agreement to replace VAMA was the outcome of those discussions. The agreement is a voluntary partnership between the two organizations to identify fair housing issues, concerns, and solutions.

The agreement incorporates a strong local emphasis whereby both NAR and HUD will encourage the development of similar local partnerships between HUD field offices and NAR state and local associations. Members are encouraged to adopt a Fair Housing Declaration that incorporates a commitment to a broad set of fair housing principles. The agreement continues VAMA's emphasis on voluntary compliance and education, but shifts the focus to joint actions that address issues.

Along with a fair housing "Guide," NAR sent each local association executive officer a copy of the "Model Affirmative Fair Housing Marketing Plan." The model plan includes the Fair Housing Declaration and a series of actions for members to use to meet the HUD requirements.

6

Legislation for the Disabled

Antidiscrimination and "equal access" legislation for the disabled is primarily set forth in the Americans with Disabilities Act of 1990 (ADA) and in California Civil Code §§54–55.1: Blind and Physically Disabled Persons.

The ADA prohibits discrimination against individuals with disabilities within the spheres of employment, public services, telecommunications, public accommodations, and commercial facilities. Its provisions cover two broad areas—accessibility and employment—where people with disabilities have faced obstacles. The ADA has far-reaching effects on employers, building owners, and businesses, since it requires owners and tenants to make their properties accessible.

Civil Code Section 54

The parallel state law, Civil Code Section 54, mandates that individuals with disabilities are entitled to full and equal access. This includes common carriers, public accommodations and buildings, streets, sidewalks, highways, telephone facilities, housing accommodations, rentals, private schools, and lodging places. "Full and equal access" must meet the standards of Titles II and III of the federal Americans with Disabilities Act of 1990.

◼ Definition of Disability

According to the ADA, a condition is a "disability" if it "substantially limits one or more of an individual's major life activities." Specific disabilities include impairment of sight, hearing, or mobility, HIV infection, dyslexia, epilepsy, alcoholism, and various mental and emotional conditions. This list may be expected to change as the law evolves.

Disability per the Rumford Act

The Rumford Act defines physical disability as including "any physiological disease, disorder, condition, cosmetic disfigurement, or anatomical loss that affects one or more major body systems (neurological, immunological, musculoskeletal, respiratory, cardiovascular, reproductive, etc.)."

"Mental disability" includes mental retardation, emotional or mental illness, and other disorders. It does not apply to the unlawful use of controlled substances or drugs.

■ Employment Impacts

There are an estimated 16 million persons who have been unable to find work due to discrimination against a disability. Title I of the ADA prohibits discrimination in employment.

Prohibited Acts under ADA

When an employer limits, segregates, or classifies an applicant or employee in a way that affects opportunities or status because of disability, it constitutes discrimination, whether intentional or not.

Examples include:

- Exclusion from jobs on the basis of disability unless the ability in question is an "essential function" of the job
- Failure to make "reasonable accommodations" for disabled workers, such as modifying building access, equipment, schedules, etc., unless the business can show that it would experience "undue hardship"
- Using testing or assessment procedures that exclude those with physical, sensory, or mental handicaps, unless the ability the test is measuring is an essential job function
- Asking about a job applicant's disability or requiring pre-employment medical examinations
- Discriminating against a person who is related to or associates with a disabled person.

Employers Affected

Implementation of Title I was required as of July 26, 1992, for employers with 25 or more employees and as of July 26, 1994, for employers with 15 to 24 employees. For real estate offices, "employees" include salespeople classified as independent contractors. "Employers" include all businesses except Native American tribes and certain nonprofit organizations. Government employers are covered separately in Title II.

Qualifying as Disabled

A "qualified individual with a disability" is a person with a disability who, with or without reasonable accommodation, can perform the essential functions of the job in question.

Workplace accommodations include ramps, Braille markings in elevators, voice-activated computers, and desks and partitions placed with adequate room for wheelchair users.

■ Access to Public Facilities

ADA Title III

Title III applies to "public accommodations and services," which cover almost all business establishments, including professional offices, transit depots, etc. Title III's central thrust is that a business may not deny persons the opportunity to participate in or benefit from the business's goods, services, or facilities on the basis of disability.

Physical accessibility standards are established for new construction and alternations in "places of public accommodation and commercial facilities." Both landlord and tenant are responsible for access to a building.

Modifications to Property

The federal Fair Housing Act of 1988 requires landlords to reasonably accommodate special needs of disabled persons. This includes allowing tenants to make certain structural modifications to the property at the expense of the tenant. New construction of four or more units intended for occupancy since March 13, 1991, must be designed to be accessible by mobility-impaired persons.

Tax Credit for Compliance

There is a Disabled Access Tax Credit for small businesses for 50 percent of "eligible access expenditures" up to $10,000 (with a $250 deductible), and a deduction up to $15,000 per year for removal of architectural and transportation barriers.

Hardship exemption.   Failure to make "reasonable" modifications in policies, facilities, or services is considered discrimination, unless the entity can demonstrate that modifications would cause undue hardship or fundamentally alter the nature of the business. Removal of architectural, communication, and other barriers is required where it is "readily achievable."

Residential rental exemption.   The ADA does not include rental housing among "public accommodations." The 1988 amendments to the Federal Fair Housing Act, however, require landlords to make reasonable accommodations, such as permitting tenants to install ramps and other devices, and further require that new construction of four or more units be accessible.

California Civil Code provisions.   Civil Code Section 54 entitles disabled persons full and equal access to housing accommodations. "Housing accommodations" means any real property used or occupied as the home, residence, or sleeping place of one or more human beings, except hotels and similar businesses, or any single-family residence where not more than one room is rented.

Property modifications.   The law does not require a landlord to modify the property in any way or provide a higher degree of care for an individual with a disability than for an individual who is not disabled.

Guide dogs.   It is a denial of equal access to housing accommodations to refuse to rent to an individual because the individual uses the services of a guide, signal, or service dog, or to refuse to permit an individual with a disability to keep such a dog on the premises. The terms of a rental agreement, however, may regulate the presence of dogs on the premises. The law does not relieve a tenant from liability for property damage caused by the dog.

Financial status.   It is a denial of equal access to housing accommodations to refuse to rent to an individual with a disability on the basis that the individual is partially or wholly dependent upon the income of his or her spouse, if the spouse is a party to the lease or rental agreement. This does not, however, prohibit a lessor or landlord from considering the aggregate financial status of an individual with a disability and his or her spouse.

Example

Assume a person with multiple sclerosis cannot work full-time and depends on his wife's income for support. This disabled person may not be legally denied an apartment with his wife simply because he is dependent on her for support.

■ Enforcement and Penalties

ADA Enforcement

Legal remedies provided in the act are pursued by private civil action and include attorney's fees, hiring, reinstatement, back pay, court orders to stop discrimination, modification of facilities, and damages.

If there is a pattern of discrimination, the attorney general may prosecute, and civil penalties may be imposed up to $50,000 for a first violation and up to $100,000 for each subsequent violation.

The administrative agencies for enforcement are the Equal Employment Opportunity Commission for Title I and the Department of Justice for Titles II and III. The law encourages "alternative means of dispute resolution" instead of litigation.

Enforcement—Section 54

Section 54.3 provides that any person or business that interferes with the rights of an individual with a disability under this law is liable for damages for each offense, up to three times the amount of actual damages but in no case less than $250, plus attorney's fees as determined by the court.

■ Unit 6 Review Quiz

1. The primary thrusts of federal and state legislation for the disabled are to prohibit discrimination and provide equal access to public facilities.

   a. True
   b. False

2. An applicant for employment states in the job application that she has been an alcoholic and has been treated for depression stemming from drug abuse. Although highly qualified for the job, the applicant is rejected. Based on these circumstances alone, the applicant may have grounds to claim discrimination.

   a. True
   b. False

3. A 20-unit apartment building was constructed in San Jose in 1998. The complex had only limited access for mobility-disabled persons. Under California law, the owner

   a. is exempt from disabled-access requirements because the properties are homes.

   b. is exempt because tenants are primarily month-to-month renters.

   c. need only provide limited access for properties built after the 1997 deadline.

   d. has violated California Code Section 54.

7

Fair Credit and Credit Reporting Laws

Antidiscrimination laws in residential financing focus on equal credit opportunity and rules for accessing private credit reports.

The Principal Fair Credit Laws

- The federal Equal Credit Opportunity Act of 1975
- The Holden Act (California Health and Safety Code §§35800–35833)

The Principal Fair Credit Reporting Laws

- The federal Fair Credit Reporting Act
- The California Consumer Credit Reporting Agencies Act (CCCRAA) (Civil Code §§1785.1–1786.56)

■ Fair Credit Laws

ECOA

The federal Equal Credit Opportunity Act became effective on October 28, 1975. It prohibits lenders from discriminating against credit applicants and requires that a lender or creditor who denies an application must provide the applicant with a statement of reasons or a written notification of the applicant's right to a statement of reasons.

The Holden Act

The Holden Act was enacted to prevent discrimination in the financing of residential real estate. In passing the Holden Act, the California Legislature declared that a healthy housing market allowing residents a choice of housing opportunities in a free market place is necessary to the state's economy and the health, safety, and welfare of its residents.

Additional Aims of the Holden Act

The Holden Act (known as the Anti-Redlining Act) aims to:

- Encourage lending in areas where conventional financing has been unavailable
- Increase the availability of housing to creditworthy persons
- Ensure the supply of decent, safe housing
- Prevent the abandonment and decay of neighborhoods

■ Prohibitions

ECOA's Prohibited Discrimination

Under ECOA, it is unlawful for any creditor to discriminate against any applicant with respect to any aspect of a credit transaction

- based on race, color, religion, national origin, sex, marital status, or age; or
- because all or part of the applicant's income derives from public assistance; or
- because the applicant has in good faith exercised any right under the ECOA.

Holden's Prohibitions

Under the Holden Act, lending institutions are prohibited from the following forms of discrimination:

- Refusing to lend due to neighborhood trends (redlining)
- Discriminating against individuals or properties in the availability of financing
- Appraising using neighborhood trends based on changes in race, color, etc.

Applicability   This act applies to one- to four-unit properties to be used as the owner's residence. It also applies to home improvement loans, even if the owner will not occupy the property. The law provides penalties and legal remedies for violation.

Exceptions, Special Programs, and Exemptions to Prohibitions

Marital status, age, and public assistance qualifications.   Under ECOA, a creditor *may* inquire into and consider:

- Marital status, if the purpose is limited to ascertaining the creditor's rights and remedies and is not related to creditworthiness
- Age or public assistance, if the purpose is to determine the amount and probable continuance of income or other matters relevant to creditworthiness
- Age, in order to use an empirically derived credit system that considers age, if the system is demonstrably and statistically sound
- Age of an elderly applicant, if age is to be used by the creditor *in favor* of the applicant

Neighborhood conditions.   Under the Holden Act, neighborhood conditions may be considered if "the financial institution can demonstrate that consideration of these conditions in the particular case is required to avoid an unsafe and unsound business practice."

Special purpose program exceptions.   Under ECOA, creditors are permitted to restrict eligibility for loan programs under certain circumstances.

Examples include programs that are:

- Expressly authorized by law for an economically disadvantaged class of persons
- Administered by a nonprofit organization for its members or for an economically disadvantaged class
- Offered by a profit-making organization to meet special social needs

Under Holden, there is no prohibition against special loan programs, provided they are designed to promote housing opportunities in ethnic minority or low-income neighborhoods.

A second exception is that a loan need not be granted if it facilitated an occupancy that would create an imminent threat to the health or safety of the occupant.

The Holden Act does not preclude lenders from considering the fair market value of the property.

Federal institutions exemption.   Court decisions have established that federal regulation of federal savings and loan associations "is now so pervasive as to leave no room for state regulatory control." Therefore, the redlining prohibition of the Holden Act cannot be applied to them.

Notification of Outcome

Under ECOA, a creditor must notify the applicant of its action within 30 days after receipt of a completed application.

If credit is denied, the applicant is entitled to a statement of reasons from the creditor.

The creditor may comply by:

- Providing a written statement of reasons for adverse action as a matter of course along with the notice of adverse action
- Including with the notice of adverse action a disclosure of the applicant's right to request a statement of reasons, and the name of the person or office from which the statement is obtained

The Holden Credit Denial Disclosure Act of 1976 mandates essentially the same disclosure provisions for affected state lenders.

Enforcement and Penalties

ECOA.   The Federal Trade Commission (FTC) is the primary enforcement agency for the ECOA. The injured party may bring action in U.S. District Court or any state court of competent jurisdiction within two years of the violation.

Remedies may include:

- Actual damages, court costs, and attorney's fees
- Punitive damages not greater than $10,000
- Equitable and declaratory relief to enforce compliance with the law
- Discovery proceedings concerning the creditor's credit granting standards

Holden act enforcement.   The Secretary of the Business, Transportation, and Housing Agency oversees lending practices of financial institutions.

Within 30 days of receipt of a complaint, if the secretary investigates and finds that a financial institution has engaged in an unlawful practice, the secretary may issue a cease and desist order, and either

- order the institution to make the loan on nondiscriminatory terms, or
- award damages to the complainant if the loan is no longer available.

The secretary may also recommend to the state treasurer that state funds not be deposited in a financial institution in violation of this law.

Importance of Credit Reporting Laws

The objective of the federal Fair Credit Reporting Act (FCRA) is "to insure that consumer reporting agencies exercise their grave responsibilities with fairness, impartiality, and a respect for the consumer's right to privacy."

The California Consumer Credit Reporting Agencies Act (CCCRAA) closely parallels the Federal Fair Credit Reporting Act. Its aim is to regulate consumer credit reporting in order to protect the rights of the people of California. At the same time, it recognizes that "extension of credit is a privilege and not a right."

Permitted Uses of Reports

Under FCRA, consumer-reporting agency may furnish reports only to users investigating the individual in connection with:

- Credit transactions
- Employment
- Insurance
- License issued by government
- Other "legitimate business need"
- Court order
- Consumer's written request.

Exclusions and Time Limits

Under the FCRA, adverse information such as bankruptcy, liens, judgments, and convictions may not be reported if they antedate the report by more than seven years (ten years for bankruptcy), *except* when the amount of the credit or insurance is $150,000 or more, or the employment is at an annual salary of $75,000 or more.

Disputed Information

Under both the FCRA and CCCRAA, a consumer may dispute the accuracy of information in the file, and the agency must investigate. If the information is found to be inaccurate, it must be deleted, and the consumer may request that corrected reports be sent to recent recipients. If the information remains in dispute, the consumer may file a brief statement that becomes part of the record, unless the agency deems it "frivolous or irrelevant."

Disclosure to the Consumer

The FCRA requires that the consumer be notified whenever an investigative consumer report "may be made." The consumer then has the right to disclosure of "the nature and scope of the investigation."

The investigating agency must disclose:

- The nature and substance of all nonmedical information about the consumer in its files at the time of the request
- Sources of information (with exceptions)
- Recent recipients of reports on the consumer

Enforcement

Under the FCRA and CCCRAA, consumers may pursue damages for an agency's noncompliance with this law within two years of the violation. Otherwise, no consumer may bring any action for defamation, invasion of privacy, or negligence against any consumer reporting agency, user, or provider of information, except for false information furnished with malice or willful intent to injure.

Damages may include actual damages, punitive damages up to $5,000, and court costs and attorney's fees.

Home Mortgage Disclosure Act. Congress enacted the Home Mortgage Disclosure Act in 1975 (HMDA) and the Federal Reserve Board's Regulation C implements the law. The period of 1988 through 1992 saw substantial changes to HMDA. Especially significant were the amendments to the act resulting from the Financial Institutions Reform, Recovery, and Enforcement Act of 1989 (FIRREA). The law expanded coverage to include many independent nondepository mortgage lenders, in addition to the previously covered banks, savings associations, and credit unions. The Federal Deposit Insurance Corporation Improvement Act of 1991 further expanded coverage of independent mortgage bankers.

As the name implies, HMDA is a disclosure law that relies upon public scrutiny for its effectiveness. It does not prohibit any specific activity of lenders, and it does not establish a quota system of mortgage loans to be made in any Metropolitan Statistical Area or other geographic area s defined by the Office of Management and Budget.

Financial institutions must report data regarding loan originations, applications, and loan purchases, as well as requests under a preapproval program if a preapproval request is denied or results in the origination of a home purchase loan. HMDA requires lenders to report the ethnicity, race, gender, and gross income of mortgage applicants and borrowers. Additionally, lenders must identify the type of purchaser for mortgage loans that they sell.

■ Unit 7 Review Quiz

1. Under California fair lending laws, mortgage lenders may decline residential financing in an area based on projected deteriorating values, provided the denial is based on a legitimate appraisal survey sanctioned by the DRE.

   a. True
   b. False

2. A lender refuses to lend funds to an unmarried woman with three children. Since the bank in fact inquired as to the applicant's marital status, the bank has violated fair lending laws.

   a. True
   b. False

3. Under the provisions of the Holden Act, mortgage loan underwriting is a confidential process wherein lenders may opt not to disclose the reasons for an applicant's rejected application.

   a. True
   b. False

4. A consumer claims a violation of CCCRAA has occurred. She wanted to buy a $1,500 computer on credit. The store had a credit report run, and it accurately disclosed numerous loan defaults and a bankruptcy three years ago. Subsequently, the store refused her credit. Based on the provisions of CCCRAA, the consumer most likely

   a. has a legitimate claim against the reporting agency for disclosing the bankruptcy.

   b. has a strong claim against the store for ordering the credit report.

   c. has grounds for action against the reporting agency for issuing the report at all.

   d. has no case whatsoever because the report was justified, accurate, and legitimate.

5. A consumer discovered that, upon applying for an apartment rental, the reporting agency had furnished the landlord with a credit report containing a previous rent payment default. The payment had been made, but the report, by accident, had not been corrected. Unfortunately, the problem occurred over two years ago. When the landlord rejected the application in favor of another tenant, the consumer was simply out of luck.

   a. True
   b. False

Fair Housing and Practices Laws

HUD Regulations: Advertising

- Code of Federal Regulations spells out detailed advertising guidelines for the fair housing logo, poster, publisher's notice, and use of human models
- Logo or slogan "Equal Housing Opportunity" must be displayed
- Real estate advertising section must be introduced with publisher's notice of nondiscrimination
- Human models in display ads must be representative of community "in an equal social setting"
- Failure to display poster is evidence of discrimination, if a complaint is filed

Americans with Disabilities Act, 1990

- Prohibits discrimination on the basis of physical or mental disability
- Affects employment, public accommodations, services, businesses, communications, etc.
- Employment discrimination includes failure to make reasonable accommodations and exclusion based on disability when not related to essential job functions
- Access to public accommodations: virtually all businesses must make "reasonable" accommodations unless they would cause undue hardship or fundamentally alter the nature of the business
- Buildings must be accessible effective 1992–93
- Does not cover rental housing, but the Fair Housing Act 1988 Amendment requires new multiunit housing to be accessible
- Enforcement by private civil action; attorney general may prosecute repeat offenders

■ Blind and Physically Disabled Persons—Civil Code Sections 54–55.1

- Added to Civil Code in 1968 to ensure full and equal access to businesses, services, etc.
- Guide dogs must be permitted on premises; exception for animal parks
- Listening and transcription devices must be provided in court on request

■ California Consumer Credit Reporting Agencies Act

- Closely parallels the federal Fair Credit Reporting Act
- Seven-year time limit on adverse information
- Consumer may dispute information; agency must investigate and correct or allow consumer to file a statement
- Remedies include actual and punitive damages, costs, and fees; actions for defamation and invasion of privacy generally barred

Unit 2 Review Answers

1. **b.** Housing discrimination, and real property discrimination in general, continued through the use of restrictive covenants.
2. **a.** While numerous other California laws prohibited housing discrimination, the Rumford Act took particular aim at discrimination in the workplace as well.
3. **d.** Under the DRE's Section 2780, no licensee may discriminate in the sale of any property, including residential, commercial, andindustrial properties, or the agent's own property.
4. **c.** Fair housing laws ban discrimination against all American citizens, whether they are in a protected class or not; you do not have to "join" one to enjoy the law's protection. Further, since Adam was not rejected for financial reasons, it appears he may have a legitimate complaint that could be pursued.
5. **b.** A violation has in fact occurred, since the advertising used is discriminatory. Owners are no longer exempt from fair housing law if they discriminate in advertising or hire an agent.
6. **b.** Complainants may file suit in court at both federal and state levels for violations of antidiscrimination law, regardless of the findings of HUD's administrative law judges.

Unit 3 Review Answers

1. **a.** On face value, it could be argued by the first offeror that the owner had given a secret instruction to the agent not to sell to nonwhites, since the owner accepted a lower offer only three days later. Therefore, both owner and agent could be in violation of fair housing laws.
2. **d.** As a licensee, Michael is prohibited from representing someone who has indicated a desire or motivation to discriminate. Therefore, he should respectfully refuse the listing from his father.
3. **c.** The ad, however subtly, seeks to interest older prospects. It disparages people with young children; it promotes quietness and gentle forms of transportation; and it excludes younger people who do not have grandchildren. Unless the agent is promoting bona fide senior housing—which is doubtful since a single house is being promoted—the agent is liable for age discrimination in advertising.
4. **b.** There is insufficient information to make the determination. Although it might appear that the agent discriminated in favor of the Caucasian, it could easily be true that both prospects barely qualified in May, and that the banks raised their lending requirements in November, disqualifying them both.
5. **c.** The landlord cannot legally require intensified screening for applicants simply because they are black or Hispanic, regardless of their employment history.

6. **a.** The agent is liable for possible steering since he identified a Hispanic neighborhood as the best location, while subtly disparaging other areas, Hispanic or otherwise, based on the assumption that the prospect would prefer a Hispanic neighborhood.

7. **d.** Since the original policy was discriminatory, the agent cannot be reprimanded or terminated for refusing to comply. Moreover, the manager is now liable for retaliation as well as discrimination.

Unit 4 Review Answers

1. **b.** Displaying the poster is an affirmative statement of the firm's compliance with antidiscrimination laws. It does not shield one from paying too much for a property or otherwise agreeing to "unfair" terms of a transaction.

Unit 6 Review Answers

1. **a.** The ADA is not limited to access issues, but also extends to providing the disabled with equal employment opportunity.

2. **a.** The applicant's disabilities from alcohol and depression are covered by the ADA, even though her drug abuse is not.

3. **d.** The owner has committed a violation, since the complex is a nonexempt housing accommodation that must be accessible according to Section 54 provisions.

Unit 7 Review Answers

1. **b.** The Holden Act provides no such exemption in prohibiting residential financing based on a neighborhood's projected decline in value.

2. **b.** Lenders may inquire as to one's marital status provided the justification is based purely on the rights and remedies of the lender with respect to such marital status, as opposed to creditworthiness. Further, the bank's rejection may be based on an evaluation of the applicant's financial capabilities irrespective of marital status.

3. **b.** The Holden Act provides for exactly the opposite, that all applicants have a right to the lender's disclosure of reasons why a loan application received adverse action.

4. **d.** The store was within its rights, the reporting agency was within its rights, the report was accurate (no complaints were made about that!), and the bankruptcy was disclosable.

5. **a.** The consumer had no recourse against the reporting agency since two years had elapsed without correcting the mistake, and the agency had acted without malice in reporting an erroneous report.

Course 4: Trust Fund Handling

Introduction to Trust Fund Handling

Real estate licensees commonly receive trust funds in the normal course of business. Transactions involving trust funds and trust fund account handling include real estate sales, property management, broker escrows, and mortgage load brokerage.

The California Department of Real Estate reports that trust fund mishandling is the second most common type of enforcement problem after misrepresentation. The mishandling of trust funds ranges from the inadvertent placement of trust funds into the broker's general account to the intentional conversion of a client's money for the broker's personal use.

The real estate law and the regulations of the real estate commissioner establish legal requirements for receiving and handling trust funds. This course reviews the requirements and illustrates the precautions a licensee should take to ensure the integrity of trust fund accounts.

Basics of Trust Fund Handling

General Responsibilities

Trust Funds

A trust fund is something of value received by an agent on behalf of a principal and held for the principal's benefit. The "thing of value" can be cash, a check, a personal note, or tangible or intangible personal property, whether the instrument is made payable to the broker, a seller, or a neutral escrow depository.

Almost all funds received by real estate licensees are construed as trust funds. Deposits and other funds that an agent accepts on behalf of another fall into this category.

Brokers and salespersons must handle, control, and account for these trust funds according to established legal standards. Improper handling or accounting can result in serious business consequences, civil liabilities, or revocation or suspension of a real estate license.

Nontrust Funds

Funds that are not construed as trust funds include commissions, general operating funds, and rents and deposits from *broker-owned* real estate. These "nontrust funds" are not subject to the trust fund handling provisions of the real estate law and Commissioner's Regulations, and they must not be commingled (mixed) with trust funds.

Fiduciary Responsibility

In almost every real estate transaction, an offeror gives something of value to an offeree as a "good-faith deposit." This item of value is entrusted temporarily to the care and handling of a licensee. As a result, the licensee has a fiduciary responsibility to the owners of such funds. This fiduciary duty requires the licensee to handle the funds according to the law and to use them only for purposes authorized by the owners.

When the transaction has yet to be completed, and throughout the transaction, it is necessary to determine who owns the money, as ownership of the funds controls how the funds are handled.

Need for Exact Records

The licensee must maintain an accurate, complete, and up-to-date accounting of trust funds. Trust fund record-keeping violations often accompany trust fund mishandling. Compliance with money handling and record-keeping requirements is necessary to protect the sanctity of the trust account and prevent the broker from drawing upon the money as if it belonged to the broker.

■ General Procedure

A typical trust fund transaction begins with the broker or salesperson receiving trust funds from a principal in connection with the purchase or lease of real property. A real estate salesperson must either immediately deliver the funds to the broker or, if directed by the broker, place the funds in one of the other manners described below.

In order to comply with Business and Professions Code Section 10145, and as Commissioner's Regulation 2782 requires, not later than three business days following receipt of the funds by the broker or broker's salesperson, trust funds must be placed into

■ the hands of the broker's principal (written instructions are required from all principals to do so),

■ a neutral escrow depository, or

■ a trust fund bank account pursuant to Commissioner's Regulation 2830.

Escrow Depository

A neutral escrow depository, as used in Business and Professions Code Section 10145, means an escrow business conducted by a person licensed under Division 6 of the Financial Code or by any person described in Section 17006 of the Financial Code. Generally, this includes financial institutions, title companies, attorneys, and escrow companies.

Exception: Deposit Checks

Commissioner's Regulation 2832 also provides that the broker may hold a deposit check uncashed until acceptance of the offer under the following conditions:

■ The check is not negotiable by the broker (that is, not made payable to the broker), or the offeror has given written instructions that the check shall not be deposited or cashed until acceptance of the offer.

■ The offeree is informed, before or at the time the offer is presented for acceptance, that the check is being so held.

If the offer is later accepted, the broker may continue to hold the check undeposited only with written authorization from the offeree.

Otherwise, the check must be placed, not later than three business days after acceptance, into a neutral escrow depository, or into the trust fund bank account, or into the hands of the offeree if *both* the offeror and offeree expressly so provide in writing.

■ Determining Ownership

Since only the person who owns the trust funds may authorize their disposition or distribution, it is imperative for the broker to identify who actually owns the funds *at any point throughout a transaction*. The initial owner of the money is the party who gave the funds to the licensee. Ownership may change during the transaction, depending upon the terms stated in the contractual instructions.

Ownership of a Deposit in an Offer

Ownership of funds deposited with the licensee in connection with an offer depends upon whether the offer has been accepted by the offeree.

Before acceptance, the funds belong to the offeror, and they must be handled according to the offeror's instructions, whether deposited into a trust account or held uncashed until acceptance of the offer.

After acceptance, the offeror is no longer the sole owner of the funds, and the funds must be handled according to instructions from the offeree:

■ The offeror's check may continue to be held uncashed after acceptance only upon written instructions from the offeree.

■ The deposit in a real estate sales transaction may not be refunded to the offeror without the express written consent of the offeree.

If a check has been held uncashed in accordance with the offeror's written instructions, Commissioner's Regulation 2832(d) may apply: "if the offeror's check was held by the broker in accordance with subdivision (c) until acceptance of the offer, the check shall be placed into the hands of the offeree if offeror and offeree expressly so provide in writing not later than three business days following acceptance of the offer unless the broker receives written authorization from the offeree to continue to hold the check."

■ Unit 2 Review Quiz

1. A trust fund always consists of funds received in the form of cash or a check.

   a. True

   b. False

2. At four o'clock on a Friday afternoon, Ms. Collins hands agent Apfelbaum a check as an earnest money deposit with her signed offer to purchase a house. In the absence of further instructions, which of the following action *must* agent Apfelbaum take?

   a. Deposit the check in his own trust fund account that same day

   b. Hold the check until receiving instructions from the seller

   c. Immediately deliver the check to the broker

   d. Open an escrow account within 24 hours

3. Ms. Collins's offer to purchase a home is rejected by the seller. She requests the broker to return her deposit check immediately. Before he can do this, however, the broker must obtain the seller's authorization to release the funds.

   a. True

   b. False

Advance Fee Trust Funds

Some brokers collect fees from clients in advance to cover the cost of services that are to be performed on their behalf, such as promoting the sale of property or arranging a loan. Advance fees are trust funds that belong to the principal, not the agent. These funds must be submitted, collected, deposited, accounted for, and treated according to procedures prescribed in the Business and Professions Code and the real estate law.

It is not unusual for advance fees to be charged in the sale or lease of real estate, but they are most common in the loan brokerage business. Funds received in connection with mortgage loan brokerage are subject to additional regulations (see Unit 9 of this course).

■ Definition of "Advance Fee"

Section 10026 of the Business and Professions Code defines an *advance fee* as money that is "claimed, demanded, charged, received, collected, or contracted for a listing, advertisement, or offer to sell or lease property, other than in a newspaper of general circulation, issued primarily for the purpose of promoting the sale or lease of business opportunities or real estate, or for referral to real estate brokers or salespersons, or soliciting borrowers or lenders for, or to negotiate loans on, business opportunities or real estate."

Section 10026 was amended so as not to include rental application fees, or "screening fees," so long as such fees do not exceed $30 per applicant plus CPI (consumer price index) increases since 1998.

■ DRE Approval Requirements

When brokers decide to solicit or charge advance fees, all material used in the solicitation must be submitted to the real estate commissioner in advance for approval.

B&P Code: Solicitation Materials

Section 10085 of the Business and Professions Code requires that all materials such as contract forms, letters, and advertisements be submitted for approval at least ten days prior to use. Use without approval is a misdemeanor with a penalty of up to $1,000 fine and six months in jail, plus DRE disciplinary action.

Real Estate Law: Advance Fee Agreements

Commissioner's Regulation 2970 in the Code of Regulations requires that advance fee agreements be submitted for approval at least ten days prior to their use of collection of any advance fee. The agreements must be printed in at least ten-point type.

The commissioner will deny approval of an agreement under any of the following conditions:

- The agreement is misleading or deceiving, or contains misrepresentations.
- The agreement does not fully describe the services to be rendered for the advance fee.
- The total amount of the advance fee is not stated, or the date that it is due and payable is not stated.
- The agreement contains provisions that relieve the broker from fulfilling any commitments or representations made by the broker's agents or employees in soliciting such fees.
- The agreement purports to guarantee financing of the real estate or business opportunity as a result of services rendered for the advance fee.
- The agreement does not state the date for full performance of the services secured by the advance fee.

■ Record-Keeping Requirements

Advance fees are trust funds. They are not the broker's funds, even though they are collected to pay the broker. Until they are disbursed, they remain the funds of the principal from whom they were collected. They must be deposited into a trust account, and they must be accounted for in a manner consistent with other kinds of trust funds. Section 10146 of the Business and Professions Code allows the commissioner to regulate the method of accounting for advance fees.

Duty to Principal

Section 10146 also provides that principals of advance fee trust funds are to receive verified copies of the accounting of their funds from the broker at the end of each quarter and/or at completion of their contract with the broker. Should any funds be misapplied, the principal is allowed treble damages for the amounts, plus reasonable attorney fees.

Receipts

Commissioner's Regulation 2972 establishes the accounting requirements for advance fees. Accounting for advance fees received must include:

- The names of the agent and the principal
- The amount collected
- Identification of the trust account into which the fees were deposited
- A description of the services rendered or to be rendered for that fee

Disbursements

When disbursements are made from the account, the amount of disbursement must be allocated in the accounting for each of the following:

- Disbursements for each service listed in the description of services rendered or to be rendered
- Disbursements to pay commissions to agents and representatives
- Disbursements to pay for costs and profit

Special Requirements: Advertising

When disbursements have been made for advertising, the accounting must include a copy of the advertisement, the name of the publication in which it appeared, the number of advertisements actually published, and the dates that they appeared.

Special Requirements: Loans

In mortgage lending, when an advance fee is for the arrangement of a loan on real estate or a business opportunity, the accounting must list the names and addresses of persons to whom the broker submitted the principal's loan portfolio, along with the dates of submittal.

■ Additional Requirements

In addition to the accounting requirements and disbursement disclosures, other regulations apply to broker withdrawals, auditing, and general handling procedures.

Broker Withdrawals

Section 10146 of the Business and Professions Code provides that amounts may be withdrawn for the benefit of the broker only when actually expended for the benefit of the principal, or five days after verified accounts have been mailed to the principal.

Examination by Real Estate Commissioner

The commissioner has an ongoing program to examine the broker's records to ensure that all trust fund handling and record-keeping procedures have been met.

Criminal Penalties

Sections 506 and 506a of the Penal Code describe additional violations of law that arise from failure to handle advance fees in accordance with the real estate law.

■ Unit 3 Review Quiz

1. Broker Washington decides to offer his clients special marketing services, such as listing on the Internet and advertising in national and international real estate publications. For these services, he wants an advance fee. What must he do to satisfy the Department of Real Estate regulations before he can mail out letters describing his special services?

   a. Obtain DRE approval of the letter

   b. Print the letter in ten-point type

   c. Submit the letter to the commissioner and then wait five days before using it

   d. Obtain DRE approval of the amount of the fee to be charged

2. A broker must give the owner of an advance fee trust fund a quarterly accounting of trust fund activity as well as an accounting at the end of the contract between broker and principal.

   a. True

   b. False

4

Trust Fund Bank Accounts

Trust funds must be deposited or delivered within three business days after receipt, unless written instructions authorize the broker to hold them until completion of a specified event.

If the funds are not given to the principal for whom they are intended or deposited into a neutral escrow depository, then they must be deposited into the broker's *trust fund bank account*. The broker's trust fund bank account is a segregated account that contains only trust funds belonging to principals and none of the broker's personal or business funds, other than a nominal amount allowed to maintain the account.

■ General Requirements

Section 10145 and Commissioner's Regulation 2832 requires that this trust fund bank account be designated as a trust account in the name of the broker as trustee. The account must be maintained with a bank or other recognized depository located in California, and it must not be an interest-bearing account that requires prior written notice to the financial institution before funds are withdrawn.

As with any checking account, all trust account checks should be numbered, and all voided checks should be retained. A deposit should not be returned or transferred until the deposited check has cleared the account.

■ Trust Account Withdrawals

Withdrawals from the broker's trust fund bank account may be made only upon an authorized signature on the check withdrawing the funds. The named broker bears full responsibility for the funds in the account. Commissioner's Regulation 2834 limits authorized signatures to the following:

■ The broker who is the named trustee of the account

■ In the case of a corporate broker, the designated broker-officer

- A licensed salesperson working under the broker named on the account, provided the licensee is specifically authorized to sign by the broker
- An unlicensed employee of the broker, such as a bookkeeper, controller, or accountant who is authorized in writing by the broker and who is covered by a fidelity bond equal to at least the maximum amount of trust funds to which the employee has access at any time

Trust Fund Account Protection

Broker trust fund bank accounts afford certain protections for principal funds. When legal action is taken against the broker, or if the broker becomes incapacitated or dies, trust funds held in a true trust account cannot be "frozen" pending litigation or during probate. Funds also have better insurance protection if deposited into a trust account.

Deposit Insurance

The general counsel of the Federal Deposit Insurance Corporation (FDIC), in an opinion in 1965, held that funds of various owners placed in a custodial deposit (trust account) in an insured bank are recognized for insurance purposes to the same extent as if the owners' names and interest in the account were individually disclosed on the records of the bank, provided the trust account is specifically designated as custodial and the name and interest of each owner of the funds are disclosed on the depositor's records.

Each client with funds deposited in a trust account in a federally insured bank is insured up to $100,000, as opposed to just $100,000 for the entire account, as long as the regulatory requirements are met.

An individual's trust funds will be added together with any other single-ownership funds he or she has deposited at the institution, up to a total aggregate coverage *per person per institution* of $100,000.

Interest-Bearing Accounts

Trust fund bank accounts are not normally interest-bearing accounts, but Section 10145 of the Business and Professions Code provides that they may be under specific conditions.

Specific Beneficiary

Any interest-bearing trust account must be in the name of the broker as trustee for a specified beneficiary or principal. All funds in the account must be insured by an agency of the federal government, and must be kept separate and distinct from other trust funds or broker funds.

Disclosure to Owner

The broker must disclose to the owner of the funds the nature of the account, how the interest will be calculated and paid, the account policy on service charges, and notice requirements or penalties for withdrawing funds from the account.

■ Designation of Payee

In a real estate transaction in which the broker accepts a deposit with instructions that the deposit is to be placed in an interest-bearing account, the parties must specify in writing the person to whom interest is to be paid or credited.

■ Interest May Not Go to Broker

Whatever the circumstances, interest on trust funds can *never* go to the broker or to any person licensed under the broker. Even authorization by the funds' owners cannot legally permit the broker to collect the interest on trust funds.

■ Trust Account Integrity

Trust account *integrity* means that the trust account is in order; it is properly kept with sufficient supporting records to show that all accounts balance, and there are no violations of law. To ensure that the account is so maintained, the broker must see that personal and operating funds are not commingled with trust funds. The balance of the trust fund account must equal the broker's trust fund liability to all beneficiaries, without shortages or overages. The broker must always keep the trust fund records current, complete, and accurate.

■ Trust Fund Liability

Trust fund *liability* is created by placing trust funds into a trust account. That is, the broker-trustee of the account is now liable for those funds. The amount of liability decreases as trust funds are disbursed. The *aggregate trust fund liability* at any time is equal to the total *positive* balances due to all the beneficiaries of the account at that time. If a beneficiary account has a *negative* balance, it is not deducted from the total liability, since to do so would allow the broker to be liable for less than what is due the other beneficiaries of the account.

Example

Broker Sally maintains a trust fund account that currently contains funds for three beneficiaries. The fund owes beneficiary A $10,000, beneficiary B $7,000, and beneficiary C $15,000. Broker Sally, as trustee of the account, is liable for $32,000, no matter how much money is actually in the account at the moment.

Shortage

A negative balance should not occur. If it does, it is a *trust fund shortage*, which means that the total balance in the trust fund account is below the total trust fund liability. This situation typically occurs when the broker disburses trust funds belonging to other beneficiaries on behalf of a beneficiary who has inadequate funds at the time to cover the disbursement. This is a violation of Commissioner's Regulation 2832.1, unless the broker has received prior written authorization from *all* beneficiaries of the account to reduce the balance below the total liability.

Example

If broker Sally in the previous illustration paid out $8,000 to cover some obligation of beneficiary B, she would be disbursing $1,000 of funds that do not belong to B, and there would be a shortage of $1,000.

This is violation of Commissioner's Regulation 2832.1, unless the broker has received prior written authorization from *all* beneficiaries of the account to reduce the balance below the total liability.

Overage

On the other hand, if the trust account balance is *greater* than the total trust fund liability, there is a *trust fund overage*. An overage is also a violation of real estate law, since it must be a result of commingling, unless the overage falls within the limited cases that temporarily allow personal funds to be in the trust account.

Precautions

A trust fund discrepancy of any kind is a serious violation of the real estate law. Many broker and sales licenses have been revoked after a DRE audit disclosed a trust account shortage, even where the shortage had been corrected prior to the audit. To ensure that the balance of the trust account at all times equals the trust fund liabilities, a broker should take the following meticulous precautionary measures:

- Deposit trust funds in a timely manner
- Allow funds to clear the account before making disbursements
- Never allow a beneficiary's account to be negative
- Maintain accurate, current, and complete records of trust account activity

■ Unit 4 Review Quiz

1. Broker Adams is licensed in both California and Nevada. When he receives trust funds from clients, he generally deposits them in his Nevada trust fund account. This practice will not get him in trouble in California unless he has failed to obtain written permission from the commissioner of real estate.

   a. True
   b. False

2. Which is a feature of the broker trust fund account?

   a. The account is insured by the FDIC for up to $100,000.
   b. The broker is named as the beneficiary of the trust in an interest-bearing account.
   c. It cannot be an interest-bearing account.
   d. The funds remain available to owners even if the broker dies or is sued.

3. What is it that the broker must always keep equal to maintain trust account integrity?

   a. The aggregate of deposited funds and the FDIC insurance amount
   b. Aggregate trust fund liability and account balance
   c. Shortages and overages for each individual beneficiary
   d. The aggregate trust fund liability and the total positive balances due to all the beneficiaries of the account at that time

Trust Fund Violations

■ Commingling

Commingling is a "mixing" of personal funds with trust funds, or a *failure to separate* trust funds from personal and business funds. Although commingling is not the same as stealing the trust funds, it is a misdemeanor. Commingling may result in the suspension or revocation of the broker's real estate license. The following acts by the broker are construed as commingling under the real estate law.

Failure to Deposit by Three Business Days

Unless otherwise instructed in writing by the owner of the funds, trust funds received must be deposited within three business days into either a trust fund bank account or a neutral escrow depository. Failure to do so is considered commingling and is a violation of the real estate law.

Personal Funds

Depositing personal funds into the trust fund bank account is a violation even if separate records are kept.

Broker-Owned Property

A common infraction of these rules occurs when a broker deposits rents, security deposits, purchase deposits, or mortgage payments from principals on *broker-owned* properties into the trust fund bank account. Since these deposits are for properties owned by the broker, the transactions are considered "personal business," and depositing these nontrust funds into a trust account is commingling.

Exceptions

There are only two cases where personal funds may be in a trust fund account.

1. *Service charges.* The broker may keep no more than $200 of personal funds in the account for the purpose of covering bank charges for maintaining the account. To avoid problems, a better practice is to have the institution withdraw such charges from the broker's personal or business account. In any case, service charges cannot be paid from trust funds.

2. *Commissions and fees.* The broker may have income earned and collectible from the funds in the trust account, such as commissions or fees collectible out of rents and mortgage payments. Fees to the broker must be withdrawn from the trust account within 25 days from the date they are earned, but they cannot be withdrawn until the funds providing for payment of the fees have been deposited. The broker may not pay a personal obligation from the account against fees due the broker from the account, but must first withdraw the fee and *then* pay personal obligations from personal funds.

Deposit in Nontrust Account

If trust funds are deposited into an account of the licensee's other than the trust account, the violation can be even more serious than commingling if intent to take the trust funds is established.

Failure to Withdraw

Commingling also occurs when commissions, fees, or other earned income that is collectible from the trust account remain in the account after 25 days from the date earned.

■ Trust Fund Conversion

Conversion is deliberate misappropriation of trust funds, or more bluntly, stealing the funds. While commingling is a misdemeanor, conversion is defined by Section 506 of the Penal Code as a form of embezzlement—a felony. It is one of the most serious offenses a licensee can commit while acting as a fiduciary.

DRE Disciplinary Action

Any licensee guilty of trust fund conversion will ultimately lose his or her real estate license. The administrative procedure for revoking a license begins with the DRE presenting a formal accusation of the charge of conversion according to the Administrative Procedures Act. The real estate commissioner is the complainant, and the licensee is the respondent to the charge.

Procedure.   The hearing is conducted by an administrative law judge from the Office of Administrative Hearings The commissioner's case is presented by the commissioner's counsel, and the judge makes a proposed decision based on the findings. The commissioner issues an official decision, accepting or rejecting the judge's proposed decision. If the charges are upheld, the commissioner will most likely call for forfeiture (revocation) of the license.

Appeals.   If the respondent disagrees with the decision based on the evidence, he or she may petition for reconsideration and then has the right to appeal to the courts. After a license is revoked, the person affected may not apply for reinstatement of the license until one year has passed. Reinstatement may or may not be granted.

Receivership

When a licensee is convicted of trust fund conversion, receivership may be instituted by the court in a manner similar to that used in bankruptcy. Since the licensee has embezzled clients' funds by spending or otherwise combining them with the licensee's own funds, action must be taken to freeze the licensee's assets in order to find and recover the stolen trust funds. Assets may eventually be sold or otherwise recovered in order to reclaim the embezzled trust funds.

Bankruptcy

If a licensee has converted trust funds and then becomes insolvent, the problem is complicated by creditors of the bankruptcy also claiming the assets of the broker. Since the trust funds were never the rightful property of the insolvent licensee, they are not subject to the creditors' claims. The converted trust funds must be identified and are considered stolen property. Eventually, when recovered and separated from the assets of the bankruptcy, they must be distributed by the courts to the rightful owners.

Civil Liability

When a broker receives trust funds, he or she becomes liable for the funds until they are disbursed to the rightful parties. A broker who has committed conversion is civilly liable to the owners of the funds converted. The broker can be sued to recover the funds from the broker's personal and business assets. Any and all assets of the licensee may be legally "attached" pending the outcome of the lawsuit, so they can be liened if judgment is rendered against the licensee, and, if necessary, sold in order to satisfy the judgment.

Tax Implications

A question of tax liability may arise when a broker commits trust fund conversion. Normally, since the broker is only a custodial agent of trust funds and has no ownership of them, he or she incurs no income tax liability from handling them. But when the broker embezzles the funds, they become income in the eyes of the Internal Revenue Service. Should the broker escape detection or prosecution for conversion, he or she becomes liable to the IRS to report the converted funds as income and to pay tax on them. The IRS considers *any* income as reportable income, regardless of its source.

Criminal Prosecution

A licensee who has converted trust funds is guilty of embezzlement, which is a felony. When the evidence is sufficient to warrant criminal prosecution, the district attorney in the county where the offense took place will approach the grand jury for an indictment, and the licensee will be tried in a criminal court. The DRE will act as a witness for the prosecution if the commissioner believes that the licensee has committed conversion.

Penalties.   Once convicted of conversion in the criminal court, the licensee will be subject to a fine, imprisonment, or both. Conviction could easily result in a fine in excess of $1,000 *and* imprisonment in excess of one year.

■ Unit 5 Review Quiz

1. Broker Jefferson has some personal funds from earned property management fees in a trust fund account. The funds were deposited two weeks ago and the checks have cleared. Broker Jefferson wants to pay some service personnel who work for him on the property he manages. Even though the service people actually work for the benefit of the property owner, broker Jefferson cannot pay them with a check drawn against the trust fund account without violating a regulation.

   a. True
   b. False

2. What is the primary distinction between commingling and conversion?

   a. Commingling may result from accident or carelessness, while conversion is the result of an intent to steal.

   b. Conversion may lead to revocation of the license to practice real estate.

   c. The Department of Real Estate enforces the law against commingling, but the enforcement of the law against conversion is entirely in the hands of the criminal justice system.

   d. Commingling is not considered a serious offense.

6

Trust Fund Accounting

Properly kept records enable the broker to:

- Prepare an accurate accounting for clients
- Determine the amount of money the broker owes account beneficiaries
- Prove whether or not there is an imbalance in the account
- Prove that funds in the trust account belong to beneficiaries only
- Guarantee beneficiaries that all amounts in the trust fund are insured by FDIC coverage

Accounting for all trust funds accurately and regularly requires use of a consistent accounting system.

The accounting system must meet the following DRE criteria:

- All receipts and disbursements must be detailed in chronological sequence.
- The balance of each trust fund account must be calculated based on recorded transactions. Tracing the recorded steps taken by the broker in handling each account must lead to an accurate, up-to-date balance of the account.
- The system must present in chronological sequence all receipts and disbursements that affect each beneficiary account.

■ Accounting Systems

Two kinds of accounting systems for trust accounts are acceptable to the Department of Real Estate. They are *columnar records*, as prescribed by Commissioner's Regulations 2831 and 2831.1, and *noncolumnar records* that are in accordance with generally accepted accounting practices. The broker is free to choose whichever system is most suited to the broker's operations.

Columnar Records

The columnar record option requires keeping the following records in a columnar format. Various forms may be used, depending on the situation.

- Columnar Record of All Trust Funds Received and Paid Out—Trust Fund Bank Account Record (DRE Form RE 4522, referred to in this course as BAR)

- Separate Record for Each Beneficiary or Transaction (DRE Form RE 54523, referred to in this course as SBR)

- Record of Trust Funds Received but Not Deposited to the Trust Fund Account (DRE Form RE 4524, referred to in this course as RUR)

- Separate Record for Each Property Managed (Form RE 4525, referred to in this course as SPR)

Record of All Trust Funds Received and Paid Out (BAR)

The BAR form is used to journalize all trust funds deposited to and disbursed from the trust fund bank account. At a minimum, it must show the following information in columnar form:

- The date funds were received
- The name of payee or payor
- The amount received
- The date of deposit

- The amount paid out
- The check number and date
- The daily balance of the bank account

All transactions affecting the bank account are entered in chronological sequence on this record regardless of payee, payor, or beneficiary. If there is more than one trust account, a separate record must be maintained for each account, pursuant to Commissioner's Regulation 2831.

Separate Record for Each Beneficiary or Transaction (SBR)

This form is maintained to account for the funds received from or for the account of *each* beneficiary or for *each* transaction. With these records, the broker can identify the funds owed to each beneficiary or transaction at any time. The wording is "each beneficiary or transaction," because some trust fund deposits are not permanently identifiable as belonging to a specific beneficiary, as in the case of a purchaser's deposit in a sale. The record must show in chronological sequence in columnar form:

- The date of deposit
- The amount of deposit
- The name of payee or payor
- The check number, date, and amount of the check

- The balance of the individual account on any date
- Dates and amounts of interest earned and credited to the account, if applicable

A separate SBR must be maintained for each beneficiary or transaction from whom the broker received funds that were deposited into the trust fund bank account. If the broker has more than one trust fund bank account, then each account must have its own set of separate beneficiary records so that they can be reconciled with the individual trust fund bank account record.

Record of Trust Funds Received But Not Deposited (RUR)

This form is used to keep track of funds received but not deposited into a trust fund bank account, as when the broker is instructed by the principal to hold a check uncashed for a period of time, or when the broker receives a check made out to another party as a deposit on a purchase. It must show:

- The date funds were received
- The form of payment (check, note, etc.)
- The amount received
- A description of property involved
- The identity of the person to whom the funds were forwarded
- The date of disposition of the funds

Trust fund receipts are recorded in chronological sequence, while their disposition is recorded on the same line where the corresponding receipt is recorded. Transaction folders or files showing the receipt and disposition of undeposited checks are *not* acceptable alternatives to the required use of this form.

Commissioner's Regulation 2831(e) exempts from recording requirements the handling of "pass-through" checks on a total not to exceed $1,000 created by a principal in a particular transaction made out to third party payees, for the provision of services (e.g., escrow, credit, and appraisal services).

Separate Record for Each Property Managed (SPR)

This form is similar to the separate record for each beneficiary or transaction form and serves the same purpose when a trust fund account is for rental properties. It need not be used if all the information is already contained in the separate beneficiary record form, but it is useful when the broker wants to show detailed information about a specific property being managed.

Noncolumnar Records

When a non-columnar accounting system is chosen, it must be in accordance with generally accepted accounting practices and must include at least the following records:

- *Journals* recording chronologically all trust fund transactions
- *Cash ledger* showing the bank balance as affected by the transactions recorded in the journals, posted in a debit-credit format
- *Beneficiary ledger of each account* showing chronological transactions affecting each beneficiary's account and the balance of each account

Journals.   Journals are a daily chronological record of trust fund receipts and disbursements. A single journal may be used to record both receipts and disbursements, or a separate journal may be used for each.

Besides recording all trust fund transactions in chronological sequence, the journal must contain sufficient information to identify the transaction, such as the date, amount received or disbursed, name of payee or payor, check number or reference to another document of the transaction, and identification of the beneficiary account affected. Journals must show the total receipts and total disbursements *regularly,* but at least once a month.

Cash ledger.   The cash ledger shows the periodic increases and decreases (debits and credits) in the trust fund bank account and the resulting account balance. It can be incorporated in the journals, or it can be a separate record. If a separate record is used, *the postings must be based on the transactions recorded in the journals;* that is, the amounts posted on the ledger must be those shown in the journals.

Beneficiary ledger. A separate beneficiary ledger must be maintained for each beneficiary or transaction or series of transactions. This ledger shows in chronological sequence the details of all receipts and disbursements related to the beneficiary's account and the resulting account balance. It reflects the broker's liability to a particular beneficiary. *Entries in these ledgers must be based on the entries recorded in the journals.*

Relation of ledgers and journals. The journals must correlate with the ledgers, showing the same figures that are posted, individually or in total, in the cash ledger and in the beneficiary ledgers. *The details in the journals must be the basis for posting on the ledgers and arriving at account balances.*

Recording Process

Specific procedures should be adopted and followed routinely in order to keep complete, accurate, and current trust fund records. Transactions should be recorded daily in the trust fund bank account and in the separate beneficiary records. Consistent source documents should form the basis for recording receipts and disbursements.

Example

In real estate sales, trust account receipts should be recorded, based on a purchase contract and receipt for deposit form, and disbursements will be recorded from checks from the trust fund bank account.

Balancing

It is advisable to calculate the balance for each beneficiary or property account on all applicable records at the time any entry is made. This eliminates having to dig back into the records to find an error made several entries ago. The records should also be reconciled (matched against the bank statement) monthly to ensure that trust account transactions are properly recorded on both the bank account record and the applicable record for the transaction.

Multiple Accounts

If more than one trust fund bank account is maintained, a separate set of properly labeled columnar records is required for each trust fund bank account.

Reconciliation of Accounting Records

The trust fund bank account record, the separate beneficiary or transaction or property record, and the bank statement are all interrelated. Any entry made on the bank account record (BAR) must have a corresponding entry on a separate beneficiary record (SBR) of separate property managed record (SPR). Similarly, any entry or transaction shown on the bank statement must be reflected on the bank account record (BAR). This applies to columnar record systems as well as to other accounting systems.

Monthly Reconciliation

The accuracy of the records can be verified by doing a reconciliation at least once a month. **Reconciliation** is the process of comparing two or more sets of records to determine if their *balances agree*. This process will disclose whether or not the records are completed accurately. For *trust fund record keeping*, two reconciliations need to be made at the end of each month:

1. Reconciliation of the bank account record (BAR) with the separate beneficiary (SBR) or transaction or property records (SPR), *required by Commissioner's Regulation 2831.2*

2. Reconciliation of the bank account record (BAR) with the bank statement, which is *not required by law or regulation* but is an essential step in maintaining an accurate accounting system

Reconciliation #1. This reconciliation will verify that all transactions entered on the bank account record were posted on the separate beneficiary, transaction, or property managed records; that is, that all entries on the bank account records are accounted for to the separate records of specific transactions. The balance on the bank account record should equal the total of all beneficiary and property record balances. Any difference should be located and the records corrected to reflect the correct bank and liabilities balances.

- This reconciliation is required on a monthly basis, except in months when there is no activity in the trust fund bank account.

- A record of each reconciliation must be maintained in the broker's record for at least three years.

- This record should identify the bank account name and number; the date of the reconciliation; the account number or name of the principals, beneficiaries, transactions, or properties; and the trust fund liabilities of the broker to each of the principals, beneficiaries, transactions, and properties.

Reconciliation #2. Reconciliation of the bank account record with the bank statement will disclose any recording errors by the broker or the bank. If the balance on the bank account record agrees with the bank statement balance after adjusting for outstanding checks, deposits in transit, and other transactions not yet shown in the bank statement, there is additional assurance that the bank account record is correct. Although this reconciliation is not required, it is crucial in assuring accuracy.

Reconciliation Guidelines

For either of these reconciliations, some procedural guidelines should be followed.

Effective date. Prior to beginning a reconciliation, make sure that *all* records are current and all transactions are recorded up to the cut-off date of the bank statement. Use the balances shown on the beneficiary or transaction, bank account, and property managed records as of the last day of the bank statement. All the trust fund records are now "in sync" with each other and with the bank statement.

Adjusted bank balance. For bank account reconciliation, calculate the "adjusted" bank balance from the bank statement and the bank account record. This is done by adding to or subtracting from the bank statement those entries on the bank account record that have not yet shown up on the statement, such as a check that has not yet cleared. The balances of the bank account record and the bank statement are now "in sync."

Discrepancies.   Any differences between the various sets of accounting records should be located and corrected immediately. Discrepancies can be caused by not recording a transaction, recording an incorrect figure, erroneous calculation of balances, missing beneficiary records, and bank errors.

Retention of records.   Records of the reconciliations performed at the end of each month, along with the supporting documents, must be kept for at least three years.

■ Unit 6 Review Quiz

1. In the columnar accounting system, the general record of deposits, withdrawals, and account balance is recorded on the:

    a. SBR form.

    b. RUR form.

    c. PDR form.

    d. BAR form.

2. In a noncolumnar accounting system, receipts and disbursements in the journal must be totaled at least quarterly.

    a. True

    b. False

3. In both the columnar and noncolumnar accounting systems, for every entry in the record of the general account, there must be a corresponding entry in a

    a. passbook account.

    b. manual or computerized spreadsheet.

    c. separate beneficiary or transaction record.

    d. DRE database.

4. Both of the monthly reconciliations in the columnar system require comparing various records with the bank statement.

    a. True

    b. False

5. What should you do if you find a discrepancy between the bank account record, the bank statement, and the separate beneficiary records?

    a. Alert the bank manager

    b. Send a exculpatory letter to the commissioner

    c. Wait until the following month to see if the discrepancy corrects itself

    d. Locate the cause immediately and correct it

unit seven

7 Trust Fund Documentation

■ Activity Documentation Requirements

In addition to accounting records, the Department of Real Estate also requires the broker to maintain other documents prepared or obtained in connection with any real estate transaction.

The following are various types of trust fund activity transactions that are normally handled by a licensee, along with the supporting documents the licensee should retain.

Type of Transaction	Documents Needed
1. Receiving trust funds:	1.
a. Purchase deposits from buyers	a. Real estate purchase contract and receipt for deposit form
b. Rents and security deposits from tenants	b. Collection receipts (receipt book stubs)
c. Other receipt	
2. Depositing trust funds	2. Bank deposit receipts
3. Forwarding buyers' checks to escrow	3. Receipt from escrow company and copy of check
4. Returning buyers' checks	4. Copy of check signed and dated by buyer showing receipt of check
5. Disbursing trust funds	5. Canceled checks and, where applicable, all paperwork supporting disbursement of funds

Type of Transaction	Documents Needed
6. Receiving offers and counteroffers from buyers and sellers.	6. Real estate purchase contract and receipt for deposit; agency and transfer disclosure statements
7. Collecting management fees from the trust fund bank account	7. Property management agreements between the broker and property owners; canceled checks
8. Reconciling bank account record with the separate beneficiary records	8. Reconciliation record

Contracts Involving Licensed Activities

Under Business and Professions Code Section 10142, any time a licensee prepares or has prepared an agreement authorizing or employing that licensee to perform any acts for which a real estate license is required, when the licensee obtains the signature of any person to any contract pertaining to such services or transaction, the licensee must deliver a copy of the agreement to the person signing it at the time the signature is obtained.

Examples are:

- Listing agreements
- Real estate purchase contracts
- Receipt for deposit forms
- Addenda to contracts
- Property management agreements

Broker Supervision

Commissioner's Regulation 2725 requires that every instrument prepared or signed by a real estate salesperson in connection with any transaction for which a real estate license is required, and that may have a material effect upon the rights or obligations of a party to the transaction, shall be reviewed by the salesperson's broker.

Delegation

As long as the broker does not relinquish overall responsibility for supervision of salespersons, the broker may delegate this responsibility to any broker or salesperson licensed to the broker who has entered into a written delegation agreement with the broker. A salesperson so authorized must have at least two years' full-time experience as a sales licensee during the preceding five years.

Broker Escrows

In any real property or business opportunity transaction where an escrow is conducted by a real estate broker, the broker's responsibility to review instruments extends to escrow instructions and closing statements prepared or signed by a salesperson licensed to the broker or by an associate or employee of the broker, if rendered to the parties prior to close of escrow.

■ Unit 7 Review Quiz

1. In addition to maintaining proper accounts and performing monthly reconciliations, the broker must maintain copies of all relevant receipts, canceled checks, disbursement records, and agreements in order to comply with the regulations for handling trust fund activity.
   a. True
   b. False

Audits and Examinations

Because of the importance of trust fund handling, the commissioner has an ongoing statewide program of examining brokers' records. Licensees who are audited will be made aware of trust fund handling and record-keeping requirements where necessary. During the course of an audit or examination, if trust fund imbalances are uncovered or money handling procedures pose a potential for monetary loss, disciplinary proceedings will be initiated, even if a loss has not yet occurred.

■ Purpose

The general purpose of the audit program is to improve the performance of real estate brokers, especially in relation to their handling of clients' funds. The DRE uses audits to:

■ Weed out flagrant violators through disciplinary action

■ Correct minor infractions and educate brokers whose activities are otherwise acceptable

■ Substantiate the performance of those whose activities are in compliance with regulations

Thus the DRE can better assure the public of competent and safe handling of their transactions.

■ General Requirements

Section 10148 of the Business and Professions Code provides that a licensed real estate broker shall retain, for three years, copies of all listings, deposit receipts, canceled checks, trust records, and other documents in transactions for which a real estate broker license is required. The retention period runs from the date of the closing of the transaction or from the date of the listing if the transaction is not consummated.

■ Access for Audit

Upon notice, books, accounts, and records must be made available for examination by the commissioner or representative during regular business hours. Upon the appearance of sufficient cause, records shall be subject to audit without further notice, except that an audit shall not be harassing in nature.

■ Initiation of Audit

Auditing can be at random or in response to a written complaint to the DRE. When a bona fide written complaint is received, the department will investigate. If it determines that an audit would be appropriate to arrive at the truth, it will order an examination of the broker's records. Over time, the audit has proven to be one of the most productive tools of the DRE for resolving complaints and determining whether there has been wrongdoing by licensees.

■ Results of Audits

By their nature, audits and examinations seek to determine whether violations of law and regulations have occurred. The findings will either absolve the licensee of any wrongdoing or confirm violations. If violations have occurred, the action taken against the licensee will depend on the nature, number, and severity of the violations.

The law allows the DRE to charge for the costs of an audit of a mortgage broker's trust fund records when the audit is used to establish, through an administrative hearing, that the broker has been guilty of violations.

Minor Violations

Minor or "technical" violations, such as clerical errors or a slight unintentional error in a record form, may result in a citation-warning letter, designed to prompt more meticulous efforts in the future. The licensee will be reminded that small errors, if left unchecked, may compound into more serious errors later on, regardless of how unintentional the action may have been.

Disciplinary Action

More serious violations result in an *accusation* being filed by the DRE. An accusation is an administrative procedure adopted by licensing agencies of the state. It is the first step of disciplinary action by the department. An administrative hearing is held by the DRE to confirm what violations have occurred and to what extent.

Depending on the nature and severity of the violation, disciplinary action might be:

- Suspension of the license for a stated period of time
- A monetary penalty imposed in lieu of suspension
- Revocation of the license and issuance of a "restricted" license for the remaining term of the original license
- Revocation of the license

Criminal Offenses

DRE disciplinary action addresses violations of the real estate law and the Commissioner's Regulations; that is, violations of the Business and Professions Code and the Code of Regulations. "Grave" offenses (basically, those stipulated in the Penal Code) are classified as either misdemeanors or felonies. In such cases, besides taking disciplinary action, the DRE turns over evidence of the violations to the district attorney for possible criminal prosecution. If the case is brought to trial, the real estate commissioner becomes a witness for the prosecution. Trust fund *conversion* is a felony.

■ Unit 8 Review Quiz

1. In trust fund handling, the only documents the broker must keep for three years are the reconciliation records.

   a. True
   b. False

2. When does the DRE audit a broker's trust fund records?

   a. Once a year
   b. At random, or when there is a written complaint
   c. Whenever the broker's license needs to be renewed
   d. Every three years

3. If an audit reveals a shortage in a trust fund account and further investigation reveals that the broker deliberately placed trust funds into a personal account, the broker could be prosecuted for a criminal offense.

   a. True
   b. False

Mortgage Loan Brokerage

The general trust fund handling guidelines apply to all types of trust funds held by real estate licensees. In addition, trust fund handling for mortgage loan brokers involves some requirements unique to that field. A full treatment of mortgage loan brokerage trust fund handling is beyond the scope of this course, but the following is an introduction to this specialized area.

■ Threshold Level of Activity

When a loan broker performs a certain level of business activity in mortgage lending, he or she is classified by the DRE as "threshold." Beside the regulations that pertain to all loan brokers, threshold brokers have additional reporting and disclosure responsibilities. The current "threshold" criteria are defined in Section 10232. This statute redefines the threshold mortgage broker criteria to include any broker who arranges ten or more loans with an aggregate value of $1 million of more or collects payments totaling $250,000 for private investors in a 12-month period.

Transactions involving institutional lenders (banks, savings and loans) and certain others (FHA, FNMA, GNMA, FHLMC, and USDVA) are *not* counted in establishing threshold status.

Creating or Selling Loans

Real estate–related loan transactions include creating new loans or selling or exchanging existing loans that are secured by real property or business opportunities.

Servicing Loans

Included in the threshold definition are loan brokers who service loans (collect payments from borrowers on behalf of private investors) by collecting payments totaling more than $250,000 in any 12-month period.

Intent Defined

If a broker makes, sells, or exchanges ten or more loans totaling $1,000,000 or more in any 12-month period, the law presumes broker intent to meet the threshold criteria.

■ Reporting Requirements

A broker meeting the threshold criteria must file two annual reports with the DRE within 90 days of the end of the broker's fiscal year, as well as quarterly reports.

Two Annual Reports

The first report is a review by a certified public accountant of the broker's fund financial statements.

The second is an annual report of the various aspects of the loan business conducted by the broker, DRE Form RE 881.

Quarterly Reports

Section 10232.25 requires threshold brokers to file quarterly status reports (Form RE 855) for the first three quarters of a fiscal year within 30 days of the end of each quarter. Failure to file may subject the broker to examination by the commissioner, along with a fee of one and a half times the cost of the examination and report.

A mortgage loan broker who falls short of the threshold criteria must still complete quarterly reports and keep them on file and available for inspection by the DRE.

■ Disclosure to Lenders

In addition to the threshold reporting requirements, threshold brokers must make written and signed disclosures to prospective private lenders or purchasers of an existing note when soliciting or arranging the sale of a real estate–related loan. This threshold disclosure requirement is defined in Sections 10232.4 and 10232.5, and it is part of the disclosure requirements of Article 5 of the real estate law.

■ Disclosure Content

The statement given to the prospective lender or purchaser of a note shall include the following information:

- Address or other identification of the real property
- Estimated fair market value of the securing property, date of appraisal, and name of person who made the appraisal
- Age, size, type of construction, and a description of improvements
- Identity and credit data about the borrower or borrowers, as represented to the broker
- Terms of the note
- Pertinent information concerning all encumbrances and liens against the securing property
- Provisions for servicing of the loan, if any, including disposition of late charge and prepayment penalty fees

- Detailed information concerning any proposed arrangement under which the prospective lender or purchaser, along with persons not otherwise associated with him or her, will be joint beneficiaries or obligees
- A statement of the benefits to be directly or indirectly derived by the broker, or a statement of whether the dealer is acting as a principal or as an agent in the transaction with the prospective purchaser

Multi-Lender Rules

When a mortgage loan broker funds a loan through the issuance of a series of notes of equal priority secured by the same real property, or sells undivided interests in a single note secured by the same real property to two or more persons not otherwise associated, then that loan is referred to as a "multi-lender" loan. Such loans are reported on the first page of the mortgage loan annual report. When multi-lender loans are created by a broker, additional rules apply to the trust funds.

Negative Balance

Commissioner's Regulation 2832.1 restricts negative balances for any of the beneficiaries of the trust account. When a disbursement from the trust fund bank account would create a negative balance in a beneficiary account, then the disbursement is actually coming from funds owned by other beneficiaries. Such a disbursement is allowed *only* if all the other beneficiaries of the trust fund bank account give their prior written consent.

Authority to Disburse

In multi-lender situations, the broker or authorized third party must handle disbursements to the lenders. No single investor in a note is allowed to handle any of the trust funds received for disbursement.

Proration

When payments on notes are received, all lenders must receive their prorated share of the funds, unless all lenders involved agree otherwise in writing. This prevents the broker from showing favoritism toward any one investor (lender) over another. The mortgage broker acts as a fiduciary for all investors equally.

Funding and Servicing Loans

The two primary business activities of a mortgage loan broker are to fund loans and then to service them. Though not required, it is advisable for the mortgage loan broker to maintain at least two separate trust fund bank accounts: an *escrow account* and a *servicing account*.

Escrow Account

Funds received from purchasers of notes or borrowers to pay for fee-related services are placed into the *escrow* trust fund bank account. These funds involve the funding or the sale of a loan. They are "transactional" funds; that is, the funds are necessary in performing a mortgage loan transaction, such as in the creation of a new loan or the sale of an existing one.

Examples are funds collected to pay for credit reports, appraisals, costs and expenses of loan origination, and funds received from purchasers of existing loans.

Servicing Account

A separate *servicing account* is used for depositing loan payment collections from borrowers. These funds are then disbursed to the beneficiaries of the notes. The broker must deposit any borrower funds within three business days and disburse them to the lenders as soon as the funds are verified (cleared). Article 5 of the real estate law requires written authorization from each beneficiary of a note to service the loan, and written disclosure of the fee charged by the broker for servicing.

■ Loan Service Record Keeping

When servicing loans, it is imperative that the broker maintain accurate records for each trust fund account. It is important to identify the owners of the funds so that each trust fund account transaction can be properly traced and account reports prepared. Inaccurate records run the risk of failing a trust fund audit by the commissioner.

Owner of Funds

An important fact about loan payments received from a borrower is that the *borrower* is the owner of those trust funds when deposited by the broker, and the broker's trust fund records must list that borrower as the "beneficiary" of those funds while on deposit. In other words, the borrower who pays the loan payments to the broker is the owner of the funds until they are disbursed to the lender.

Beneficiary

Confusion sometimes results from multiple meanings of the term "beneficiary." The lenders (investors in notes) are referred to as the beneficiaries of the notes (loans), but the beneficiaries of the *trust funds* are the borrowers who made the payments to the broker.

■ Unit 9 Review Quiz

1. Which broker would meet the definition of a "threshold" broker?

   a. One who collects more than $250,000 in loan payments in a 12-month period

   b. One who makes 25 loan transactions totaling $1.5 million in a 12-month period for his own account

   c. One who exchanges four loans totaling $500,000 in a 6-month period

   d. One who makes nine loan transactions totaling $900,000 in a one-year period

2. How many reports relating to loan activity and trust fund activity does a threshold broker have to file in a given year?

   a. Two

   b. Three

   c. Four

   d. Five

3. As part of the written disclosure a threshold broker must make to prospective purchasers of a note, the broker must provide an estimate of fair market value of the securing property, based on an appraisal.

   a. True

   b. False

4. Which is a "multi-lender" loan?

   a. A loan secured by several properties

   b. A loan secured by a single property in which multiple securing notes have equal priority

   c. A loan secured by several properties in which multiple lenders share an undivided interest in some of the properties

   d. A series of notes that are cosigned by multiple lenders

5. A mortgage loan broker is required to maintain two trust fund accounts, an escrow account and a servicing account.

   a. True

   b. False

6. Mary Doaks gives her monthly mortgage payment to broker Madison, who services her loan for the lender. Broker Madison deposits the payment in a trust fund. As soon as the payment is deposited, it becomes the property of the lender.

   a. True

   b. False

Sample Record Keeping

The following sample illustrates some of the procedures for keeping trust account records for typical real estate transactions occurring over a 30-day period.

Broker Hall owns and operates a one-person real estate office specializing in residential sales and property management. He has one trust fund bank account and uses a columnar record-keeping system.

■ Types of Records

Broker Hall keeps four types of columnar records for trust fund bank account activity, using the DRE forms:

1. Record of All Trust Funds Received and Paid Out—Trust Fund Bank Account, DRE Form RE 4522 ("Bank Account Record" or BAR)

2. Separate Record for Each Beneficiary or Transaction, DRE Form RE 4523 ("Separate Beneficiary Record" or SBR)

3. Record of All Trust Funds Received—Not Placed in Broker's Trust Account, DRE Form RE 4524 ("Record of Undeposited Receipts" or RUR)

4. Separate Record for Each Property Managed, DRE Form RE 4525 ("Separate Property Record" or SPR)

■ Recording Methods

Note the following points about trust fund record keeping:

- Each entry to any record shows all pertinent information on the transaction, such as date, name of payee, name of payor, amount, check number, etc.

- The daily bank balance is computed and posted on the BAR after recording transactions.

- The balance owing to the client is computed and posted on the SBR or SPR after posting transactions.

- Any entry made on the BAR has a corresponding entry on the SBR or SPR, and vice versa.

- All records except the RUR show entries chronologically regardless of transaction type. The RUR shows the disposition of a trust fund on the same line as the receipt is entered, rather than in chronological sequence.

■ Transactions

The following entries comprise the real estate activity for Broker Hall during the month. Activity is listed chronologically through the month. Each row of the activity log shows the date of the transaction, a description, the documentation required, and the entries the broker makes on the relevant forms. The forms themselves are not shown.

The following examples of trust fund records are for demonstration purposes only and do not contain all required records or documentation.

Date	Transaction	Documentation	Entries
11/1	Opened a trust account with Amalgamated Bank, and deposited $100 of broker's own money to cover bank service charges	Deposit slip prepared by broker	Record the deposit on: 1. **BAR**: balance is $100. 2. Newly prepared **SBR** for broker Hall: balance is $100
11/1	Entered into agreements to manage three properties: Address Owner Units 12 Elm St., Oak Hills Westbrook 3 156 Center St., Oak Hills O'Donnell 2 1431 South St., Oak Hills Wilson 1	Management agreements signed by property owners and broker	No entries needed at this point—no receipt, no disbursement
11/2	Received a $3,000 check payable to broker Hall from S. Newhouse as a deposit on an offer to buy a house at 1456 Cedar Drive, Oak Hills, owned by Mr. and Mrs. Farland. Buyer instructed broker Hall to hold check uncashed until acceptance by the Farlands.	Real estate purchase contract signed by S. Newhouse Collection receipt #1 issued to S. Newhouse	Enter transaction on the **RUR**. No other entries since the check was not deposited
11/4	Received and deposited rents for November from existing tenants at 12 Elm Street: **Rent** *Tenant* *Unit #* *Received* F. Tottino 3 $650 B. Simon 1 $550 E. Hammond 2 <u>$500</u> Total $1,700	Collection receipts #2, #3, and #4 issued respectively to F. Tottino, B. Simon, and E. Hammond. Deposit slip prepared by broker	Record the $1,700 receipt on the following: 1. **BAR**: balance is $1,800 2. Newly prepared **SPR** for Westbrook—balance is $1,700

Date	Transaction	Documentation	Entries
11/7	Received $2,100 from M. Sumo representing rent of $1,100 from 11/7/94 through 11/30/94 and $1,000 security deposit for 1431 South Street	Collection receipt #5 issued to M. Sumo. Receipt showed that $1,100 of the $2,100 was for rent and the other $1,000 was for security deposit. Deposit slip prepared by broker	Record the $2,100 receipt on the following: 1. **BAR**: balance is $3,900 2. *Newly prepared **SPR** for Wilson: Sumo security deposit: balance is $1,000 3. Newly prepared **SPR** for Wilson: balance is $1,100
11/7	Received and deposited rents for November from existing tenants at 156 Center Street: **Rent** *Tenant* / *Unit #* / *Received* S. Baysinger 2 $750 F. Bradley 1 $750 Total $1,500	Collection receipts #6 and #7 issued to S. Baysinger and F. Bradley respectively. Deposit slip prepared by broker	Record the $1,500 receipt on the following: 1. **BAR**: balance is $5,400 2. Newly prepared **SPR** for O'Donnell: balance is $1,500
11/10	Issued the following checks for loan payments on the managed properties: *Check* / *Payee/Prop.* / *Amount* 1001 ABC Mortgage Co. 156 Center St. $920 1002 First Western Bank 12 Elm St. $1,150 1003 HiFi Savings & Loan 1431 South St. $850 Total $2,920	Checks issued by broker. Supporting papers for each check	Record disbursements on: 1. **BAR**: balance is $2,480 2. **SPR** for: Westbrook: balance is $550 Wilson: balance is $250 O'Donnell: balance is $580
11/11	Notified by S. Newhouse that he accepted the counteroffer of the Farlands. Deposited the $3,000 check from S. Newhouse.	Real estate purchase contract with attached counteroffer signed by S. Newhouse and Mr. and Mrs. Farland. Deposit slip prepared by broker.	Record $3,000 deposit on: 1. **BAR**: balance is $5,480 2. Newly prepared **SBR** for Newhouse/Farlands: balance is $3,000 3. **RUR**—show disposition of check on record
11/15	Obtained a listing to sell a single-family house at 114 High Street, Oak Hills, owned by Mr. and Mrs. Sweet	Exclusive listing agreement signed by sellers and broker	No entries needed

Date	Transaction	Documentation	Entries
11/19	Received a $2,000 check from J. Jones made payable to broker Hall as a deposit on her offer to buy 114 High Street, with instructions to hold uncashed until acceptance	Real estate purchase contract signed by J. Jones. Collection receipt #8 issued to J. Jones	Enter transaction on **RUR**
11/21	Issued the following checks to pay for water and garbage on the managed properties: *Check*　　*Payee/Prop.*　　*Amount* 1004　Oak Hills Water Dept. 　　　156 Center St.　　$50 1005　Oak Hills Water Dept. 　　　1431 South St.　　$35 1006　Oak Hills Water Dept. 　　　12 Elm St.　　$75 Total　　　　　　$160	Checks issued by broker. Supporting papers for each check	Record disbursements on: 1. **BAR**: balance is $5,320 2. **SPR** for: 　Westbrook: balance is $475 　Wilson: balance is $215 　O'Donnell: balance is $530
11/21	Issued check #1007 for $3,000 to Only Title Co. for the account of S. Newhouse, buyer of 1456 Cedar Street	Check issued by broker. Receipt issued by Only Title Co.	Record disbursement on: 1. **BAR**: balance is $2,320 2. **SBR** for Newhouse/Farlands: balance is 0
11/22	Returned J. Jones's check to her after the sellers rejected her offer	Real estate purchase contract rejected by Mr. and Mrs. Sweet	Post the return of check on the **RUR**
11/25	Issued check #1008 for $65 to E-Z Plumbing Co. for fixing a clogged sink in unit #1 at 12 Elm Street on 11/25	Check issued by broker. Supporting paper for check	Record disbursement on: 1. **BAR**: balance is $2,255 2. **SPR** for Westbrook: balance is $410
11/30	Charged property management fees to the following accounts and issued check #1009 for $335 payable to broker Hall: **Management** *Property Owner*　　*Fee* Westbrook　　$150 O'Donnell　　$110 Wilson　　　$75 Total　　　　$335	Check issued by broker. List showing the breakdown of the check amount, showing the charge to each owner	Record disbursement on: 1. **BAR**: balance is $1,912 2. **SPR** for: 　Westbrook: balance is $260 　Wilson: balance is $140 　O'Donnell: balance is $420

Date	Transaction	Documentation	Entries
11/30	Sent statement of account to each owner of the managed properties	Bank service charge deducted from account by Amalgamated Bank. Posted 11/30 on bank statement	Record charge on: 1. **BAR**: balance is $1,192 2. **SBR** for Broker Hall: balance is $92
11/30		Reconciliation of bank statement and trust fund records	Adjusting bank balance for outstanding check for $335; bank statement and BAR agree on balance of $1,192

* Since security deposits will be accounted to the tenant in the future, broker Hall keeps a separate record for security deposits. Future entries on an **SPR** for Wilson will be on the one used for rents, unless additional security deposits are received. The total liability to the owner is the sum of the two records—one for security deposits, the other for rents and other transactions.

COLUMNAR RECORD OF ALL TRUST FUNDS RECEIVED AND PAID OUT
TRUST FUND BANK ACCOUNT

2006 Date Received	From Whom Received or to Whom Paid	Description	Received Amount Received	Received Reference	Received Date of Deposit	XX	Paid Out Amount Paid Out	Paid Out Check Number	Paid Out Date of Check	XX	Daily Balance of Trust Bank Account
11-1-06	Broker Hall	Open Trust Account	100.00		11-1-06						100.00
11-4	F. Tottino	Rent: 12 Elm St., #3	650.00	#2	11-4						750.00
11-4	B. Simon	Rent: 12 Elm St., #1	550.00	#3	11-4						1,300.00
11-4	E. Hammond	Rent: 12 Elm St., #2	500.00	#4	11-4						1,800.00
11-7	M. Sumo	Rent - #1,000, Dep - #1,000, 1431 South St.	#2,100.00	#5	11-7						3,900.00
11-7	S. Baysinger	Rent: 156 Center St. #2	750.00	#6	11-7						4,650.00
11-7	F. Bradley	Rent: 156 Center St. #1	750.00	#7	11-7						5,400.00
	ABC Mortgage Co.	Mtg. Pmt. - 156 Center					920.00	1001	11-10		4,480.00
	First Western Bank	Mtg. Pmt. - 12 Elm					1,150.00	1002	11-10		3,330.00
	HiFi S & L	Mtg. Pmt. - 1431 South					850.00	1003	11-10		2,480.00
11-7	S. Newhouse	Deposit on 1456 Cedar Dr.	3,000.00	#1	11-11						5,480.00
	Oak Hills Water Dept.	Nov. W/G 156 Center St.					50.00	1004	11-21		5,430.00
	Dept. Oak Hills Water	Nov. W/G 1431 South St.					35.00	1005	11-21		5,395.00
	Dept. Oak Hills Water	Nov. W/G 12 Elm St.					75.00	1006	11-21		5,320.00
	Only Title Co.	Deposit - 1456 Cedar Dr.					3,000.00	1007	11-21		2,320.00
	E-Z Plumbing Co.	Repair - 12 Elm St.					65.00	1008	11-25		2,255.00
	Broker Hall	Mgt. Fees - See Schedule					335.00	1009	11-30		1,920.00
	Amalgamated Bank	Nov. bank serv. chge.					8.00	SC	11-30		1,912.00

RE 4522

SEPARATE RECORD FOR EACH PROPERTY MANAGED							
Owner	Wilson			Deposit		$	
Address	1847 Wicker Blvd, Oak Hills			Monthly Rent		$	
Property	1431 South Street, Oak Hills			Commission		$	
Tenant's Name	M. Sumo			Leases		$	
Units	1			Collection		$	
Remarks	Security Deposit			Management		$	

Date	Received From or Paid To	Description	Receipt/ Check No.	Amount Received	Date Deposited	Amount Disbursed	Balance
11-7-06	M. Sumo	Deposit	#5	1,000.00	11-7-06		1,000.00

Exhibit 4a: Separate Property Record (SPR), Form RE 4525

SEPARATE RECORD FOR EACH PROPERTY MANAGED							
Owner	Wilson			Deposit		$	
Address	1847 Wicker Blvd, Oak Hills			Monthly Rent		$	
Property	1431 South Street, Oak Hills			Commission		$	
Tenant's Name	M. Sumo			Leases		$	
Units	1			Collection		$	
Remarks				Management		$	

Date	Received From or Paid To	Description	Receipt/ Check No.	Amount Received	Date Deposited	Amount Disbursed	Balance
11-7-06	M. Sumo	Rent: 11-7–11-30	#5	1,000.00	11-7-06		1,000.00
11-10	HiFi S & L	Mtg. pmt. - Nov.	1003			850.00	250.00
11-21	Oak Hills Water Dept.	Nov. W/G bill	1005			35.00	215.00
11-30	Broker Hall	Mgt. fee - Nov.	1009			75.00	140.00

Exhibit 4b: Separate Property Record (SPR), Form RE 4525

■ Reconciliation

After recording the daily transactions, the next step in the trust fund accounting process is reconciling the records at the end of the month. Broker Hall prepares the reconciliation schedules. He compares the bank balance on the BAR with the balance from the bank statement. This is the bank reconciliation. He also compares it with the total of the SBR and SPR balances. This is the control account reconciliation. In reviewing the bank statement, broker Hall sees that his bank account was debited $8 as a service charge for the month. He enters this $8 as a disbursement on both the BAR and his own SBR, so that his records reconcile.

Broker Hall Bank Reconciliation Amalgamated Bank		
November 30, 2006		
Balance per bank statement, 11/30		$2,247.00
Add deposits in transit		-0-
Less outstanding checks:		
Check #1009	$335.00	(335.00)
Adjusted bank balance, 11/30		$1,912.00
Balance per books (BAR), 11/30		$1,920.00
Less November bank service charge (to be reimbursed out of $100 broker's funds)		(8.00)
Adjusted balance, 11/30		$1,912.00

Broker Hall Bank Reconciliation Amalgamated Bank Account No. 10101-101		
November 30, 2006		
Beneficiary		*Balance*
Broker Hall	(SBR)	$92.00
Westbrook	(SPR)	260.00
Wilson / Sumo security deposit	(SPR)	1,000.00
Wilson	(SPR)	140.00
O'Donnell	(SPR)	420.00
Newhouse / Farland	(SBR)	-0-
Total per subsidiary records		$1,912.00
(Agrees with bank account record balance—BAR)		

Unit 2 Review Answers

1. **b.** The "thing of value" received for holding as a trust fund can be cash, a check, a personal note, or tangible or intangible personal property.
2. **c.** A real estate salesperson must immediately deliver the funds to the broker unless directed by the broker to give the funds to the principal or to place them in an escrow depository or trust fund account.
3. **b.** Until acceptance, the funds belong to the offeror, and they must be handled according to the offeror's instructions. Since the offer was rejected, the funds continue to belong to the offeror.

Unit 3 Review Answers

1. **a.** Material such as contract forms, letters, and advertisements must be submitted for approval at least ten days prior to use. Use without approval is a misdemeanor with a penalty of up to $1,000 fine and six months in jail, plus DRE disciplinary action.
2. **a.** Section 10146 provides that principals of advance fee trust funds are to receive verified copies of the accounting of their funds from the broker at the end of each quarter and/or at completion of their contract with the broker.

Unit 4 Review Answers

1. **b.** Section 10145 requires that the trust fund bank account be maintained with a bank or other recognized depository located in California.
2. **d.** When legal action is taken against the broker, or if the broker becomes incapacitated or dies, trust funds held in a true trust account cannot be "frozen" pending litigation or during probate.
3. **d.** The balance of the trust fund account must equal the broker's trust fund liability to all beneficiaries, without shortages or overages.

Unit 5 Review Answers

1. **a.** The broker may not pay a personal obligation from the account against fees due the broker from the account, but must first withdraw the fee and *then* pay personal obligations from personal funds. To do otherwise would be an act of commingling.
2. **a.** Conversion is deliberate misappropriation of trust funds, or more bluntly, stealing the funds.

Unit 6 Review Answers

1. **d.** The bank account record form is used to journalize all trust funds deposited to and disbursed from the trust fund bank account.
2. **b.** Journals must show the total receipts and total disbursements at least once a month.

3. **c.** The journals in a noncolumnar system must correlate with the ledgers, showing the same figures that are posted, individually or in total, in the cash ledger and in the beneficiary ledgers. Similarly, the single beneficiary records correlate with the bank account record in the columnar system.

4. **b.** The required reconciliation compares the bank account record (BAR) with the separate beneficiary (SBR) or transaction or property records (SPR); the recommended reconciliation compares the bank account record (BAR) with the bank statement.

5. **d.** Any differences between the various sets of accounting records should be located and corrected immediately. Discrepancies can be caused by not recording a transaction, recording an incorrect figure, erroneous calculation of balances, missing beneficiary records, and bank errors.

Unit 7 Review Answers

1. **a.** The Department of Real Estate requires the broker to maintain other documents, such as agreements, receipts, reconciliation reports, and canceled checks prepared or obtained in connection with any real estate transaction. The reconciliation reports must be kept for at least three years.

Unit 8 Review Answers

1. **b.** The regulations require the broker to retain for three years copies of all documents relating to transactions for which a real estate broker license is required.

2. **b.** Auditing can be at random or in response to a written complaint to the DRE.

3. **a.** The broker's actions would probably be construed as conversion, a felony. In such cases, beside taking disciplinary action, the DRE turns over evidence of the violations to the district attorney for possible criminal prosecution.

Unit 9 Review Answers

1. **a.** Loan brokers who service loans by collecting payments totaling more than $250,000 in any 12-month period fall within the "threshold" definition. B is not the answer because he "makes" and arranges the loans.

2. **d.** A threshold broker must file two annual reports with the DRE as well as quarterly reports for the first three quarters of the year.

3. **a.** The statement given to the prospective lender or purchaser of a note must include the estimated fair market value of the securing property, date of appraisal, and name of person who made the appraisal.

4. **b.** A multi-lender loan is one funded through the issuance of a series of notes of equal priority secured by the same real property or undivided interests in a single note secured by the same real property to two or more persons not otherwise associated.

5. **b.** It is advisable, but not required, for the mortgage loan broker to maintain these two accounts.

6. **b.** The borrower who pays the loan payments to the broker is the owner of the funds until they are disbursed to the lender.

Course 5: California Risk Management

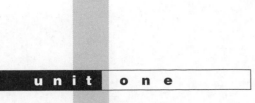

Introduction to Risk Management

As of July 1, 2007, California requires a three-hour course in risk management to renew a real estate license.

This course takes a practical approach to risk management. It covers many key laws and regulations and provides specific real-life case examples to consider.

The probability of getting sued is much higher in the real estate profession than in others, simply because of the nature of the work. For most people, real estate is the biggest investment they will make, and the transactions are complex enough to require professional assistance. Be aware that there is no way to address all possible risks involved in the practice of real estate. This course should not be considered comprehensive, but it does address a wide array of issues that licensees should keep in mind as they seek to execute their jobs properly and avoid liability.

By the end of this course, you should be able to:

- Define risk management as a concept

- Identify some major areas of real estate practice associated with high risk of liability

- Review key laws and regulations that, when obeyed to their fullest, significantly limit liability

- Recognize and resolve issues and appropriately handle situations that most frequently result in litigation

What Is Risk Management?

Risk management is a plan of action to minimize a real estate licensee's risk of liability. Risk management generally involves four components:

1. Education
2. Risk shifting

3. ~~Risk anticipation~~
4. ~~Risk control~~

Education

Legal liability has become an increasingly serious risk of doing business in real estate. Hence, real estate professionals—brokers of record as well as sales and broker associates—must not shirk their responsibility of keeping up-to-date on their education, especially with readily available resources such as the Internet, trade publications, REALTOR® associations, and books on professional development, ethics, management, and law.

Disciplinary action from the DRE and boards of REALTORS® often includes requiring the licensee or REALTOR® to attend certain educational courses, often without credit, when violations occur.

Risk Shifting

Several approaches are available to shift the risk of liability from the broker.

Errors and omissions insurance coverage. Many states require all licensees to carry mandatory errors and omissions (E&O) insurance coverage. While this insurance is not mandatory in California, it is highly recommended. Brokers should plan to devote more time and attention to risk management and their own professional liability insurance needs. To assist in this effort, here are some tips from insurance experts:

- E&O policies vary substantially among insurance carriers. It is important to consider the insured activities, exclusions, conditions, and definitions.

- Premium savings should be accomplished by taking a higher deductible, not by opting for an inadequate insurance amount. Keep in mind that the primary purpose of E&O insurance is protection against catastrophic, business-threatening lawsuits.

- Read all fine print in the policy.

- Complete the application in every detail, including information on operations, personnel, revenues, descriptive brochures, standard contracts used, résumés, and any prior claims.

- Any material misrepresentation made by an applicant for insurance, even though made innocently, whether verbal or written, renders the insurance contract voidable. A misrepresentation is a material misrepresentation when the insurance company would not have entered the contract had the complete facts been known at the time the policy was issued. The insurance company has the legal right to rescind or cancel the policy in such an event.

- Liability that may not be covered by E&O insurance includes claims based on fraud and antitrust violations.

Referring consumers to experts. Another means of risk shifting is to ensure that clients and customers get the expert advice that they need. To avoid providing negligent advice, licensees must be careful not to advise on issues in which they are not fully qualified or authorized by law to provide guidance.

To fully protect yourself, best practices would include sending a follow-up note or letter to the buyer to document instances when an agent makes a statement such as, "I am not qualified to give you an expert opinion on the condition of XYZ. A structural engineer could best answer your questions." Real estate professionals should be cautioned that if they hold themselves out to be experts in a certain trade or profession by answering questions (e.g., regarding structural soundness) they may be held to the *same performance standards* as a member of that profession (e.g., a structural engineer).

Always encourage clients and customers to consult experts for determining the condition of the property, provide a list of specialists, and create a form or disclaimer stating the choice is clearly up to the individual.

Transfer disclosure statements.   Some states require sellers to fill out property disclosure forms, while others simply recommend it. Section 1102 of the California Civil Code requires a seller of one to four residential units to provide a written disclosure of known property defects to a purchaser. Brokers are required to fill out the broker portion of the form. In terms of risk management, seller disclosure forms are a means of shifting risk from the licensee onto

■ the seller, who is obligated by law to disclose known material facts and is the person in the best position to know about any property defects, or

■ the buyer. When even the possibility of a defect is disclosed—for example, the licensee notices peeling paint and suggests the buyer have that examined for any water damage—the buyer now takes on risk if the buyer chooses not to pursue any further investigation.

Risk Anticipation

Risk anticipation involves identifying the source of problems and taking steps to ensure that such problems do not arise. Many lawsuits involve similar issues, such as misrepresentation of property condition, or improvements that were made without conforming to building codes. By knowing the areas of risk, licensees can anticipate potential issues and act to avoid problems.

This course is devoted to covering some potential areas of risk so that licensees can best anticipate issues and avoid problems.

Risk Control

Brokers should establish procedures to identify the first signs of a grievance and set up written policies to deal with a complaint before it goes to litigation.

Licensed associates and office staff should be required to immediately report the first clues of a buyer's dissatisfaction or "buyer's remorse" to the broker or a designated manager.

All sales associates and office staff should be made aware of the importance of answering any complaint with respect and consideration, no matter how unfounded it may appear.

Prompt action by the broker is essential, showing understanding but emphasizing the positive points of the property. In the case of buyer's remorse, it may be necessary to sell the property all over again. Often, an expert opinion may lay a buyer's concerns to rest.

If the firm is responsible for the issue and likely to incur liability, the broker and his or her attorney may consider the possibility of a settlement rather than risk litigation.

■ Risk Management and the Consumer

With the remarkable growth of the Internet, buyers and sellers are often arriving to first meetings with licensees armed with a great deal of information. However, the information is not always reliable, and, even when accurate, it can be misleading. A seller, for example, might be able to quote median home prices in California but not recognize that market values differ markedly from one city, or even from one neighborhood, to another.

With so much data available publicly, the real estate professional's role is constantly changing, and licensees should be aware that they will be expected to sort out bad information from good information and provide the analysis and specific experience that will be of value to educated and uneducated consumers alike.

It is important that licensees list the sources of the information they provide to consumers and only use reliable sources that have been thoroughly vetted.

■ A Note About Law

Risk management would be much easier if there existed a simple set of tasks that a licensee could follow to avoid all risk. Certainly, there are tasks—how and when to disclose an agency relationship, for example—that must be followed to avoid severe penalties. But the real world is far more complicated than simply following a predetermined set of guidelines.

First, there are many laws out there. There are federal statutes, state statutes, regulatory agency rules at both the federal and state levels, municipal ordinances, and more.

Because laws can often be open to interpretation, court decisions based on certain laws can change the complexion of an existing requirement. In many instances, these decisions clarify the law and establish clear standards for licensees to follow. But, they don't always have the desired effect. Law can be a gray area.

It is not always clear to what standard a licensee will be held when sued. As noted above, if a licensee provides some advice outside his or her area of expertise, the licensee might well be held to the same standard as an expert. While the general principle for issues like misrepresentation involves comparison to a "reasonable person," that's a flexible standard. One judge or jury might have a very different concept of what a "reasonable person" would believe. Also, some courts have held licensees to the standards of the National Association of REALTORS®, even if the licensee is not a member.

Licensees acting as agents have a fiduciary relationship with their principals. This is a high legal obligation that should be taken very seriously. It includes the duties of obedience, loyalty, disclosure, confidentiality, accounting, and reasonable care and skill. The "reasonable" care and skill is often the element most likely to be claimed in a legal proceeding, as it is flexible. The standard of what constitutes "reasonable" care can also then be determined by the "reasonable person" standard.

There is a general principle in law that when two regulations related to the protection of the public conflict with each other, the higher standard prevails. It is highly recommended that licensees err always on the side of protecting the public and interpret laws and court rulings and any notion of a "reasonable person" with that same caution.

■ Recommendations

- ■ Stay up-to-date on any changes to law. Seek out educational opportunities to stay on top of best practices in risk management.

- ■ Do not try to save on errors and omissions insurance policies by reducing the benefit. Increase the deductible instead.

- ■ Be sure to have sellers fill out Seller Property Disclosure forms, and encourage them to fill in everything they know about the property that might reasonably be considered a defect to a buyer. It is far better for the seller to disclose a problem than to risk future legal action.

- ■ Licensees should speak with their supervising broker to go over any office policies regarding dealing with unhappy members of the public. Learn to listen well for signs of displeasure.

- ■ Recognize how consumer expectations are changing in regard to real estate licensees. Make sure you learn and communicate the source of all information you disseminate.

- ■ Interpret laws and regulations from the perspective of protecting the public. It is better to be strict in applying ambiguous regulations.

■ Unit 1 Review Quiz

1. Purchasing errors and omissions insurance permits the broker to transfer financial risk to the insurance company.

   a. True
   b. False

2. In order to contain E&O costs, brokers may want to consider lower insurance coverage.

   a. True
   b. False

3. When asked about the condition of the building foundation, a wise agent will respond,

   a. "It looked fine to me."
   b. "That is beyond my expertise; you probably should discuss this with a qualified engineer."
   c. "The seller has lived here for more than 20 years, and he hasn't had a problem."
   d. "I have a friend in engineering school who can give you an opinion."

4. The main purpose of E&O insurance is to

   a. reimburse the broker if a natural disaster destroys the buildings.
   b. compensate for loss of business after a disaster such as a hurricane or a flood.
   c. protect the broker against claims against the ownership of his business.
   d. protect against business-threatening lawsuits from dissatisfied clients.

5. When a buyer storms into the office complaining loudly about a problem in the house that he or she just purchased, the

   a. buyer should be told to quiet down and consult his attorney.
   b. buyer should be advised to put his complaint in writing to the real estate board.
   c. broker or manager should listen quietly and respectfully and gather information before offering any advice.
   d. seller should be advised that the buyer is unhappy and ready to sue.

Fraud, Misrepresentation, and Puffing

Misrepresentation is among the most common causes of lawsuits in the real estate profession. Many of the risk areas to be discussed in this course fall legally under the heading of fraud or misrepresentation.

■ Risk Area: Fraud, Misrepresentation, and Puffing

Fraud is intentional deceit to induce a party to act to his or her own detriment. Courts might award punitive as well as compensatory damages for an agent's fraud. In addition, fraud could result in criminal prosecution.

A licensee who showed a prospective buyer only a few units in an apartment complex probably would be implying that they were representative of all the units. If in fact the units shown were only the few updated units, the licensee's action might be considered fraud, even though specific representations were not made.

Misrepresentation is the intentional or unintentional misstatement or concealment of a material fact. Misrepresentation could result in civil damages to compensate the injured party, as well as other contractual remedies.

The case of *Ford v. Cournale* (1974) 36 C.A.3d 172 held that providing income data based on 100 percent occupancy was misrepresentation for which the broker could be held liable.

There is some question about the broker's liability to a buyer when repeating false information provided by the owner. If the broker knew or should have known the information was false, the broker likely would be liable. It is not known if the *Easton* decision (discussed on pages 192–93) would extend to a duty to check facts provided by an owner. As minimum protection, when supplying facts that have not been verified, a broker should indicate the source of the facts and that the facts have not been verified.

Puffing is considered sales talk and is a statement of opinion, such as "You will be happy in this house" or "I consider this home to be an exceptional value." There can be a fine line between allowable puffing and misrepresentation or fraud. If a licensee were to represent nearly worthless desert property as "a sound investment," a court might determine such a statement to be fraud or misrepresentation rather than mere puffing.

■ Risk Area: Unsophisticated Buyers

Court decisions seem to indicate that a licensee has greater duties when dealing with an unsophisticated party than when dealing with a sophisticated party. With an unsophisticated buyer, the licensee should ascertain that the purchaser fully understands the effect of balloon payments, points, and other matters that might not be obvious to such a buyer.

If an unsophisticated buyer requested property tax information, the licensee probably would have the duty to explain that past property taxes are not indicative of what property taxes will be in the future because the property will be reassessed upon sale.

Licensees should avoid discouraging prospective buyers from obtaining professional help, such as an attorney or a fee appraiser, and should take care not to convey a false sense of urgency. Such actions would adversely affect a broker's defense in a lawsuit involving a breach of duty or fraud.

case study

The case of *Salahutin v. Valley of Calif. Inc.* (1994) 24 C.A.4th 555 involved buyers who, in 1979, told a real estate agent that they wanted to buy a home that could eventually be divided into two lots (for each of their children). The agent found a home listed by another agent, and the MLS listing said "1 Acre+."

The agent knew that the Hillsborough property had to be at least 1 acre to allow a future lot split. In 1989, the buyers discovered that the lot contained only 0.998 acres so it could not be split. The value of the parcel was $175,000 less than it would have been if a split were possible. The court held that the selling broker had a fiduciary duty either to investigate the size of the lot or to tell the buyer he had not done so, as size was of significant importance to the buyers.

Constructive fraud can occur when the broker is merely an innocent conduit of misinformation. The court applied damages based on the value at the time of discovery of the fraud rather than at the time of purchase. (The buyers paid only $274,000 in 1979, but it would have been worth $1,100,000 in 1989 if it could have been subdivided.)

Note: If any representation by the owner or listing broker is of importance to a buyer, the selling broker should check it out or disclose to the buyer that it is the representation of another, which he or she has not verified.

■ Risk Area: Protecting Sellers from Fraud of Others

In general, the listing agent must caution the seller about any transaction in which the seller's interests are in any way endangered.

The agent must protect the principal from the fraud of others.

■ Risk Area: Predatory Lending

Predatory lending laws were enacted to protect homeowners from unfair and costly practices that stripped homeowners of their equity and often resulted in foreclosures. A loan broker who seeks to convince a homeowner to refinance repeatedly without clear benefit to the homeowner would run afoul of California's Predatory Lending Law, which applies to refinancing and home equity loans.

case study

The federal court in *U.S. v. Mayberry* (1990) 913 F.2d 719 upheld the criminal conviction of a broker. The broker arranged for his clients to purchase property and caused them to provide HUD with false information so they could obtain a federally insured mortgage. The representations included that they had made larger down payments than they actually had and that they had personally paid all settlement costs.

■ Recommendations

- Be very careful with the language you use in describing a property.
- Do not repeat information from an owner if you have any doubt about its accuracy.
- Disclose all sources of information, and let others know when you have not verified its accuracy.
- If you are working with an unsophisticated buyer, explain all issues thoroughly.
- NEVER discourage buyers or sellers from seeking professional help.
- Do not create a false sense of urgency around choices that consumers must make.

■ Unit 2 Review Quiz

1. Broker A told prospective purchasers, "You will love living in this neighborhood." After experiencing problems with their new neighbors, they sued the broker for this false statement. A court would likely determine the statement was

   a. criminal fraud.

   b. misrepresentation.

   c. puffing.

   d. None of the above

2. Intentional deceit is *MOST* closely associated with

   a. fraud.

   b. misrepresentation.

   c. puffing.

   d. None of the above

3. A listing agent for an apartment building provided data based on 100 percent occupancy of the units, when the building was not 100 percent occupied. This could be considered misrepresentation.

   a. True

   b. False

4. Licensees may be held to a higher standard of care when dealing with unsophisticated buyers.

   a. True

   b. False

Risks Associated with Conflicts of Interest

Licensees are custodians of the public trust when conducting licensed activities. Therefore, licensees may expose themselves to extreme risk whenever their interests could potentially be seen as different from the interests of the principal they represent. This lesson covers some of the most common risks associated with these conflicts of interest.

Many of these risks involve the law of agency and potential violations of an agent's fiduciary duties to a principal. Fiduciary duties include loyalty, confidentiality, disclosure, obedience (to lawful instructions), reasonable care and skill, and accounting.

■ Risk Area: Dual Agency

A **dual agency** exists when an agent represents two principals who are negotiating with each other and thus have conflicting interests. Any conduct that reasonably leads a buyer to believe that a seller's agent is representing both buyer and seller might create a dual agency.

Because agents often serve as confidants and advisors to purchasers, purchasers easily could be led to believe that the agent is representing them. To avoid the possibility of a court determination that an unintended dual agency exists, a broker must make certain that buyers fully understand that the broker might not be their representative.

While some purchase agreements state that the broker is the representative of the seller, not the buyer, this probably would not be enough to avoid a determination of dual agency if the agent's conduct has led a buyer to believe he or she was being represented.

Because of misunderstandings by buyers and sellers as to whom the agent represents and what the agency duties are, California requires the agent to provide a written agency disclosure to the parties for the sale, purchase, exchange, or lease of one to four residential units and mobile homes (Civil Code Section 2375). The listing agent can elect to be either a seller's agent or a dual agent representing both seller and buyer. Because he or she has specific duties to the seller, the listing agent cannot elect to be solely a buyer's agent. The selling agent who locates a buyer, however, can elect to be a seller's agent, a buyer's agent, or a dual agent. The listing would set forth the agency contemplated, and the purchase form would include agency confirmation.

case study

The case of *Brown v. FSR Brokerage, Inc.* (1998) 62 C.A.4th 766 involved a situation where an agent from Fred Sands Realty listed Brown's home for $2,695,000. The seller's agent orally informed Brown that he was Brown's exclusive agent. The agent told Brown that unless the price was reduced to $2.4 million, he would lose a prospective buyer. (During the negotiation process, the agent had told the seller how much the buyer was willing to offer and also told the buyer how little the seller was willing to accept, but eventually advised the seller not to accept less than a full-price offer.) While no written offer was presented to Brown, the agent said it was time to go to escrow. Brown signed, but failed to read the agency confirmation stating that the agent was a dual agent.

The superior court ruled that the agency had been properly confirmed. The court of appeal reversed, holding that a dual agency must be disclosed as soon as practical. The agency was represented as being a seller's agent, and the agent misrepresented whom he was representing until the confirmation. The court also pointed out that the agent breached duties by revealing to each party the position of the other party.

■ Risk Area: Secret Profit

An agent cannot make a **secret profit.** The agent works for the principal and is entitled only to the compensation agreed on. The fact that the principal received a good price and was treated fairly is immaterial. The principal is entitled to any secret profit the agent receives. As an example, if the agent were the purchaser through secret control of a corporation that purchased the property, the agent would have to give up the profit made on the subsequent resale. In addition, the agent would have to return any commission received because the agent breached his or her fiduciary duty.

If a buyer intends to relist the property or another property with the agent, the agent has a duty to reveal the fact that the owner's acceptance of an offer would put the agent in a position of being able to earn another commission.

case study

The case of *Roberts v. Lomanto* (2003) 112 C.A.4th 1553 involved the sale of a shopping center. Owner Roberts hired real estate agent Lomanto as exclusive leasing and sales agent. They agreed on a 2 percent sales commission for the sale of the property. When the shopping center didn't sell, Lomanto made a purchase offer of the $11 million asking price. She told Roberts the shopping center was not worth more than that. Relying on that representation, Roberts signed a sales contract with her. Before escrow closed, Lomanto requested permission to assign her purchase contract to Pan Pacific. Lomanto again told Roberts the property was only worth $11 million.

Upon close of escrow, Roberts paid Lomanto her sales commission of $110,000. Roberts later read in the newspaper that Pan Pacific had paid $12.2 million for the shopping center. Roberts sued Lomanto for fraud, breach of fiduciary duty, constructive fraud, negligent representation, and breach of contract. The superior court granted summary judgment for broker Lomanto. Roberts appealed.

The court of appeal reversed, ruling Lomanto's purchase contract did not terminate her real estate agency fiduciary duties to Roberts, or her duty of full disclosure of material facts including her $1.2 million secret profit. The appellate court ruled Roberts was entitled to $1.2 million in damages, plus exemplary damages and restoration of the sales commission.

Note: Unless the principal knows of and consents to an agent's retention of profit, profit belongs to the principal rather than the agent. It is hard to understand why the superior court gave summary judgment for Lomanto.

■ Risk Area: Referral Fees as Potential Secret Profit

When someone is moving from the area, brokers often will recommend that he or she see a particular broker in the new area. The prospective buyer reasonably could believe that the broker is acting as a gratuitous agent in recommending someone who can best meet his or her needs. This often is not the case; the broker may in fact be recommending that the buyer see a particular broker because that broker will share part of any commission upon any resulting sale. A case could be made that this fee is a secret profit being made by the presumed gratuitous agent of the buyer. If the courts agreed to this supposition, the buyer would be entitled to the secret profit paid to the referring broker. Brokers could protect themselves by making full disclosure of any financial arrangements they have with the recommended firm.

■ Risk Area: Net Listings

Under a **net listing,** the agent's commission is all money received for a property over a net amount set in the listing. Illegal in a number of other states, net listings are legal in California. However, serious conflict-of-interest problems can arise. The broker is no longer working simply to consummate a sale but wants a sale at as much over the listing price as possible. In setting the net price, the agent's best interest thus is served by as low a price as possible. That is contrary to the principal's best interests.

Prior to or at the time of acceptance of an offer on a net listing, the broker must disclose to the principal the amount of commission to be received (Business and Professions Code Section 10176(g)). If the licensee makes an extraordinary profit from a net listing, the owner may claim that the agent, in helping to set the list price, was acting in a self-serving manner and therefore breached his or her duties of financial trust. A net listing could very well be an invitation to a lawsuit.

■ Risk Area: Option Listings

In an **option listing**, the broker takes a listing combined with an option to purchase, placing the broker in the dual role of agent and principal. To exercise the option, the agent would have to reveal all offers received. This extends to oral offers as well as written ones.

Section 10176(h) of the Business and Professions Code requires the agent to reveal fully, in writing, the amount of profit and to obtain the principal's written consent to the amount of profit. The withholding of approval could prevent the exercise of the option.

In a combined listing-option agreement, the broker also should make certain that the owner understands that the exercise of the option is at the broker's discretion. The listing-option agreement is not a guaranteed sales agreement in which the broker agrees to purchase in the event a buyer is not found.

■ Risk Area: Agent as Buyer

When a licensee is acting as a principal, the licensee should inform the buyer and the seller that he or she is dealing as a principal and not in an agency capacity.

If the broker intends to purchase the property for resale, the broker should disclose not only that fact but also what the agent hopes to obtain and any possible purchasers currently known to the broker. If the agent intends to do work on the property to make the property more valuable, the agent should disclose these intentions.

In the case when a sales associate seeks to buy a property listed by the associate's broker, full disclosure could extend beyond revealing that the purchaser is licensed and is associated with the listing firm to revealing the motives or intentions of the purchaser. Many brokers will not allow any of their sales associates to purchase office listings because they feel that the firm and the purchaser also could be buying litigation.

Because the agent has the duty to represent the owner and the owner's best interests, the principal should have the opportunity to use the expertise of the agent to the principal's advantage and not have the principal's property used by the agent in a self-serving manner. In purchasing an office listing, the agent appears to be putting self-interest above the interests of a client, which violates the agent's fiduciary duties. Courts are likely to determine that an agent was acting in a self-serving manner rather than protecting the interests of the principal if there is evidence that the purchase price was substantially below market value.

If the agent helped set the list price and purchased at the list price or less and then sold at a profit, a court very likely would determine that the agent purposely set the price too low. Action such as this could result in not only compensatory damages but punitive damages as well.

Even if the owner set the list price, the agent would have a duty of financial trust to inform the owner of the property's value. If the agent accomplished a rapid resale at a profit, the courts would be more likely to determine that the agent breached his or her duty of full disclosure. The courts could determine that the agent made a secret profit, which would then have to be turned over to the principal.

When property is purchased by an agent and resold at a profit, the courts are likely to burden the agent with proving that full disclosure has been made. As a means of protection, the agent should prepare a complete disclosure of all material facts, including his or her intentions, and have it signed by the sellers prior to the purchase agreement.

Even with full disclosure, courts could determine that undue influence was used to obtain an agreement based on the principal-agent relationship of trust. Additional protection against such claims would require that the seller obtain independent legal counsel and that the seller's attorney also receive all disclosures.

Disclosures also should be made when the purchaser is related to the agent by blood or marriage or connected by a strong business or social relationship. If an appearance of impropriety exists, courts are likely to determine that a duty was breached.

Even if an agent prevails in a lawsuit, a suit by a client can damage a firm's reputation and be costly in time and money.

case study

In the case of *In re Estate of De Harte* (1961) 196 C.A.2d 452, a broker neglected to inform the administrator of an estate that the purchaser was his mother. Seventeen days after the sale was approved for $9,600, the purchaser entered into an agreement to sell the property for $11,900. The agreement was arranged by the broker. The court held that the good-faith duties of an agent preclude the agent from taking an adverse position. The court considered this sale a fraud on the court and the administrator. The sale and the prior confirmation of the broker's commission were vacated by the court.

■ Risk Area: Affiliated Business Arrangements (RESPA)

The Real Estate Settlement and Procedures Act (RESPA) is a federal loan disclosure act. While best known for requiring lenders to provide good-faith estimates and HUD information on settlement costs to loan applicants, RESPA also prohibits kickbacks. This regulation is designed to prevent real estate practitioners from earning unearned fees, potentially at the expense of the consumer. An agent may not collect a fee for referring a client to an insurance company. An exception is made for "affiliated business arrangements"; a broker can refer business to service providers in which the broker has a financial interest. However, a disclosure must be made as to charges and relationships. The broker may only receive compensation based on profit sharing of the controlled business arrangement, not based on referrals. The controlled business arrangement must function as a separate business.

■ Risk Area: Insurance Rebate Law

Title insurance companies in California must charge for services and make a sincere effort to collect such charges.

The **rebate law** extends the anticommission provisions of the Insurance Code to prohibit direct or indirect payments by a title insurer to principals in a transaction as a consideration for business. The rebate prohibition extends to any title business, including escrows.

It is a criminal offense for an employee of a title company or controlled escrow company to pay a commission (directly or indirectly) to a real estate licensee as an inducement for placement or referral of title business. The criminal penalties apply to both giving and receiving the kickback. The penalty is up to one year in jail and a fine up to $10,000 for each offense (Penal Code 641.4).

The title insurance company may, however, furnish the names of owners of record and the legal description of parcels of real estate without charge.

The California Department of Insurance has indicated that providing a broker with a "Comparative Market Analysis" is a prohibited inducement. Some title companies had given free computer software to real estate licensees. This practice violates the law unless the software relates "exclusively" to the ordering and delivery of title products and services.

■ Recommendations

- Avoid any situation that would put your interests in conflict with the interests of the person you represent.

- Make sure to follow all agency disclosure requirements. This should include informing a potential customer that you represent another at the earliest opportunity.

- Practice how to answer buyer customers' questions to make it clear you are not their representative.

- Disclose all sources of compensation. If you feel uneasy about such a disclosure, it is probably not a source from which you should be receiving compensation.

- Always disclose that you are representing a relative or close friend. Err heavily on the side of disclosure.

- Be extremely clear about and careful to follow regulations regarding referral fees, and to whom they may and may not be paid.

- Consult with your broker, and possibly legal counsel, if you are going to purchase a property you have listed.

■ Unit 3 Review Quiz

1. Which statement is *TRUE* regarding net listings?

   a. They are illegal in California.

   b. The broker must disclose the amount of commission to be received.

   c. The broker's best interests would be served by setting as high a net price as possible.

   d. None of the above.

2. Which statement is *FALSE* regarding option listings?

   a. If a property fails to sell, the broker must exercise the purchase option.

   b. Prior to exercising the option, the broker must reveal all offers received.

   c. The broker must reveal the amount of profit, if any, to the owner to exercise the option.

   d. The owner must consent in writing to the agent's profit should the option be exercised.

3. A broker sold an apartment building to a syndicate of which the broker was a member without informing the seller of this interest. Before closing, the owner discovers the broker's interest and refuses to sell. Which probably would result from a suit to collect a commission?

   a. The broker's license would be revoked.

   b. The broker would get the commission.

   c. No commission would be paid.

   d. The buyer would obtain specific performance.

4. A dual agent *MUST*

   a. tell the buyer that the seller will accept less.

   b. tell the seller that the buyer will pay more.

   c. require compensation from both buyer and seller.

   d. None of the above

4

Risks Associated with Offers, Contracts, and Trust Funds

When negotiating and creating contracts for others, licensees perform functions traditionally reserved for attorneys, but this function must be limited. Licensees must be extremely cautious to avoid the unauthorized practice of law. Whenever a transaction involves more than filling out a preprinted form approved by their brokerage's attorney or by the attorney for the principal, licensees should consult with their broker for guidance.

Licensees should be fully familiar with the preprinted contract forms they use on a regular basis, and should be sure to explain the basics of the provisions. However, if clients or customers seek explanations that go beyond the basic functions of the clauses, licensees should avoid providing negligent advice and refer the consumer to legal counsel.

Licensees should also be very familiar with the statute of frauds, which states that all contracts involving the transfer of interests in real estate must be in writing to be enforceable. (An exception is made for leases of one year or less, although it is advisable for those to be in writing as well.) It is very important that licensees heed this writing requirement during the negotiation phase of contract formation. A licensee should also be sure to understand the basic issues of contract law, including all the phases of the contract: preparation, formation, interpretation and performance, and termination.

■ Risk Area: Contracts and Unauthorized Practice of Law

A licensee could be liable for negligence in drafting an agreement and should consider this potential liability before attempting to draft any agreement or make major modifications to a printed contract. Obtaining professional legal assistance should be considered. Licensees must avoid the unauthorized practice of law. An agent's duty does not extend to giving tax advice to buyers and sellers.

case study

The case of *Carleton v. Tortosa* (1993) 14 C.A.4th 745 concerned an experienced investor, Carleton, who listed property for sale. Carleton asked the agent how many days he had to reinvest the sale proceeds. The agent told the owner to "ask your tax person." Carleton was unable to reach his accountant, but the accountant's assistant told Carleton that he had 45 days to reinvest. After the sale, Carleton learned he owed approximately $34,000 in taxes. Carleton sued the agent for professional negligence in failing to recognize a tax-deferred exchange situation. The court of appeal emphasized that a real estate agent has no duty to give tax advice. The listing statement, "A real estate agent is a person qualified to advise about real estate. If legal or tax advice is desired, consult a competent professional," strengthened the agent's defense.

Note: If the agent had given tax advice, the agent could have been found negligent and liable for damages.

■ Risk Area: Dealing with Offers

Unless expressly instructed by the owner not to present such an offer, or unless the offer is patently frivolous, every offer received, whether oral or written, must be communicated promptly to the principal. For example, offers must be presented even if received after the principal has accepted an offer and is contractually bound. The principal may wish to breach the existing contract, suffer the damages, and accept the new offer. The best rule for agents is to present all offers to the seller and let the seller decide to accept, reject, or counteroffer.

■ Risk Area: Confidential Information and Privacy Issues

The agent has a duty of confidentiality. The seller's agent could be held liable for revealing to a purchaser, without the owner's authorization, information that weakens the principal's bargaining ability. The agent's duty of confidentiality continues even after the expiration of the agency. An agent who later uses confidential information obtained through the agency relationship to the detriment of the former principal is breaching his or her fiduciary duty.

Licensees are generally privy to large amounts of private and sensitive information, such as people's personal financial situations. Licensees must use the utmost discretion in protecting this information and keeping it secure.

■ Risk Area: Offers with Subordination Clauses

A listing agent must protect his or her seller principal. There have been cases of dishonest operators who seek to trade property of dubious value or to get sellers to accept offers that are not what they appear to be and are not in the sellers' best interests. The owner must be warned about offers with **subordination clauses.** Subordination clauses allow later loans to take priority over seller financing and endanger the seller's security in the property. They allow the purchaser to wipe out the seller's security interest by placing priority liens against the property. The owner also must be warned about exchanges involving trust deeds on other properties and about any transaction in which the purchaser will end up receiving cash.

■ Risk Area: Trust Fund Handling

The broker must maintain an accurate, complete, and up-to-date accounting of trust funds. Trust fund record-keeping violations often accompany trust fund mishandling. Compliance with money handling and record-keeping requirements is necessary to protect the sanctity of the trust account and prevent the broker from drawing upon the money as if it belonged to the broker.

A typical trust fund transaction begins with the receipt of trust funds from a principal in connection with the purchase or lease of real property. A real estate licensee must either immediately deliver the funds to the broker, or, if directed by the broker, place the funds in one of the other manners described below.

According to Business and Professions Code Section 10145, not later than three business days following receipt of the funds by the broker or sales associate, trust funds must be placed into

- the hands of the broker's principal (written instructions are required from all principals to do so),
- a neutral escrow depository, or
- a trust fund bank account pursuant to Commissioner's Regulation 2830.

Exception: Deposit Checks

Commissioner's Regulation 2832 provides that the broker may hold a deposit check uncashed until acceptance of the offer under the following conditions:

- The check is not negotiable by the broker—that is, not made payable to the broker—or the offeror has given written instructions that the check shall not be deposited or cashed until acceptance of the offer.
- The offeree is informed, before or at the time the offer is presented for acceptance, that the check is being so held.

If the offer is later accepted, the broker may continue to hold the check undeposited only with written authorization from the offeree.

Once the offer is accepted, the offeror is no longer the sole owner of the funds. There have been lawsuits and many disciplinary proceedings against brokers who have returned funds to potential buyers who wanted to back out of purchase contracts.

■ Recommendations

- Do not attempt to guide people in complex areas, such as 1031 exchanges, unless you have expert knowledge on the subject.
- Seek legal advice whenever you are asked to modify a form contract.
- Never discourage buyers and sellers from consulting attorneys.
- When contracts include complex clauses, such as subordination clauses, verify that the client or customer understands the impact. Practice explaining the clause prior to meeting with the consumer.
- Follow all rules regarding handling of trust funds, making sure to meet and document all deadlines—this is among the highest risk areas for licensees.

■ Unit 4 Review Quiz

1. An agent need *NOT* disclose to an owner that he or she has received an offer when
   a. the owner has already accepted another offer.
   b. the offer is verbal.
   c. escrow has already closed.
   d. the offer is less than the listing price.

2. A listing broker may *NOT* inform a prospective purchaser that
   a. the owner will accept less than the list price.
   b. the present use of the structure does not conform to zoning.
   c. there are material defects in the improvements.
   d. the building is on filled land.

3. A prospective buyer knows that the owner is considering accepting an offer from another party. He asks you, the broker, the amount of the offer so that he can exceed it. You should
   a. tell him, because it is in the owner's best interests.
   b. tell him, because you must reveal all known facts to a buyer.
   c. notify the owner of the request.
   d. refuse to tell him or to accept any offer unless the present offer is rejected.

4. At four o'clock on a Friday afternoon, Ms. Collins hands agent Apfelbaum a check as an earnest money deposit with her signed offer to purchase a house. In the absence of further instructions, which action *MUST* agent Apfelbaum take?
   a. Deposit the check in his own trust fund account that same day
   b. Hold the check until receiving instructions from the seller
   c. Immediately deliver the check to the broker
   d. Open an escrow account within 24 hours

Risks Associated with Property Condition and Disclosures

■ Risk Area: Duty to Inspect

In the past, what an agent did not know could not hurt the agent. Agents did not want to be aware of detrimental information about a property so they would have no duty of disclosure.

Now, not only must a licensee disclose detrimental facts known about a property, but the case of *Easton v. Strassburger* (1984) 152 C.A.3d 90 determined that the licensee also has an *affirmative duty* to find out material facts. A broker's duty of disclosure applies to facts that should be known as well as known facts. In this case, a home was sold for $170,000 through a broker. After the sale, the property suffered extreme damage in a landslide. The cost to repair was estimated at $213,000.

The court held that the duties of the real estate broker include "the affirmative duty to conduct a reasonably competent and diligent inspection of the residential property listed for sale and to disclose to prospective purchasers all facts materially affecting the value of the property that such an investigation would reveal."

In this case, a reasonable inspection would have revealed the problem because testimony indicated that

■ a listing agent had seen netting on a hill used to repair a prior landslide;

■ at least one agent knew the house was built on filled land; and

■ the floor of the guesthouse was known not to be level.

California Civil Code Section 2079 et seq. was passed to codify, clarify, and modify the duties imposed by the *Easton* decision. According to the *Department of Real Estate Bulletin*, the impact of the bill can be summarized as follows:

The bill mandates only a reasonably competent visual inspection of the property. The duty to make the visual inspection is limited to residential real property of one to four units. The duty in *Easton* was limited to residential property.

It defines the standard of care owed by a broker to a prospective purchaser as the degree of care a reasonably prudent real estate licensee would exercise, and is measured by the degree of knowledge through education, experience, and examination required to obtain a real estate license under California law. *Easton* did not clearly define the measure of the standard of care owed by a broker to the buyer.

It would apply the duty only to a broker who has entered into a written contract with the seller to find or obtain a buyer and to a broker who acts in cooperation with such a (listing) broker to find and obtain a buyer. *Easton* did not limit its application to brokers with written contracts, nor did it impose a duty on cooperating brokers.

It provides that the duty of inspection does not include or involve areas that are reasonably and normally inaccessible to such inspection or to inspection of common areas in common-interest subdivisions if the seller or broker supplies the prospective buyer with the documents and information specified in Civil Code Section 1360. *Easton* did not address the issue of the scope of the inspection.

It established a two-year statute of limitations that runs from the date of recordation, close of escrow, or occupancy, whichever occurs first.

It provides that the buyer or prospective buyer has a duty to exercise reasonable care to protect himself or herself, including knowledge of adverse facts that are known to or within the diligent attention and observation of the buyer or prospective buyer. *Easton* stated that a buyer has a duty to make a reasonable inspection but did not limit its application to cases where the facts were not known but determinable by a diligent inspection or observation by the buyer.

Although not directly related to the duties imposed under *Easton*, the bill provides that no professional liability insurer may exclude, under its policy, coverage for liability arising as a result of a breach of the duty established by the bill and the *Easton* decision.

In the case of *Smith v. Rickard* (1989) 205 C.A.3d 1354, the court indicated that the affirmative duty to conduct a reasonable inspection does not extend to nonresidential or agricultural property.

■ Risk Area: Oral and Written Disclosures

The duty of a seller to disclose relevant facts concerning the property for sale can be found in California statutes, case law, and real estate regulations. Section 1102 of the Civil Code requires that a seller of one to four residential units provide a written disclosure of known property defects to a purchaser. To comply with this disclosure requirement, the California Association of REALTORS® has developed the Real Estate Transfer Disclosure Statement (TDS).

While one associates the TDS with risks having to do with disclosures, it also creates other risks that licensees should pay careful attention to. Because the TDS is a required part of a transaction, failure to provide one can allow buyers to back out of the contract. In effect, the purchase contract can become voidable.

case study

The case of *Realmuto v. Gagnard* (2003) 110 C.A.4th 193 involved two investors who signed a purchase contract to buy a residence for $683,000 with the intention of assigning the property to a Native American tribe for a casino. Because the tribe never agreed to buy the property, the buyers did not complete their purchase. The seller sued the buyers for specific performance to force the buyers to complete the purchase (the liquidated damages clause in the purchase agreement was not initialed by the parties). The purchasers responded that the seller had never delivered the TDS as required by Civil Code Section 1102 for sellers of one to four residential units.

The superior court granted summary judgment for the buyers because the TDS had never been delivered, and failure to deliver cannot be waived. The court of appeal affirmed.

"The delivery of a TDS is a nonwaivable condition precedent to the buyer's duty of performance." The buyer not requesting a TDS cannot be construed as a waiver. The court noted that after delivery of the TDS, the buyer has three days to rescind the sale.

Note: Specific performance was likely sought because the purchase price was significantly greater than the value of the property as a residence.

The disclosure of known facts includes any negative fact that would be likely to influence a purchaser's decision. The presence of minority group members in the area is not considered a detrimental fact and should not be revealed. In fact, providing such information to a buyer likely would be considered steering, which would be a violation of the Civil Rights Act of 1968.

The Real Estate Transfer Disclosure Statement is not required for business and income property. In the sale of income property or business opportunities, reliance by the buyer on false information likely could result in a lawsuit involving the broker. The broker, whenever possible, should attempt to verify figures from the owner's income tax returns and/or sales tax reports. The broker should never report income and expense figures as fact but should state that they come only from the owner and should note if and how they were verified.

■ Risk Area: Natural Hazards

The transferor of one to four residential units built before January 1, 1960, must give a buyer a booklet entitled *The Homeowner's Guide to Earthquake Safety* prior to the transfer and disclose any known deficiencies, such as absence of anchor bolts, unreinforced masonry walls, unanchored water heater, etc. The seller or his agent must also complete a **Natural Hazards Disclosure Statement** that indicates whether the property is in a special flood hazard area, an area of potential flooding, a very high fire hazard severity zone, a wildland area that may contain substantial fire risks and hazards, an earthquake fault zone, or a seismic hazard zone.

It is in the best interests of the seller as well as the buyer for the seller to disclose all potential problems of the property. Revealing possible problem areas not only alerts the buyer but also protects the seller against later claims of misrepresentation.

■ Risk Area: Revealing Death on the Premises

After three years, an agent need not disclose a death or the cause of death of a prior occupant. Civil Code Section 1710.2 states, "No cause of action arises against an owner of real property or his or her agent, or any agent of a transferee for failure to disclose the occurrence of an occupant's death upon the real estate or the manner of death where the death has occurred more than three years prior to the date the transferee offers to purchase. . . ." Licensees should disclose death by murder or suicide within three years of the sale.

Be aware that just because licensees are not required to disclose certain issues, they are not protected from a charge of misrepresentation if asked a direct question by a purchaser. Licensees should practice how to handle these situations with their broker, explaining disclosure laws while not misrepresenting facts or potentially violating the agency responsibilities to a seller.

■ Risk Area: AIDS Disclosure

Civil Code Section 1710.2 provides that neither the owner nor the agent shall be liable to the transferee for failing to disclose that an occupant was afflicted with or died of AIDS. Because the Supreme Court has held that AIDS qualifies as a disability, disclosure of AIDS could well be seen as a violation of fair housing laws.

■ Risk Area: Megan's Law

Megan's Law concerns the registration of sex offenders and making information regarding sex offenders available to the public. Civil Code Section 2079.10(a) requires that every lease or rental agreement for residential real property and every contract for the sale of one to four residential units must include a specific notice informing consumers of the available public information regarding registered sex offenders at local police and sheriff offices.

■ Risk Area: Disclosing Use Restrictions

If a licensee knows that a contemplated use is not allowed or is unlikely to be allowed because of zoning or other restrictions, the agent has an affirmative duty to tell the buyer.

■ Risk Area: Square Footage Disclosures

Licensees should be particularly cautious regarding any disclosures of square footage. Licensees should avoid any estimates of size of structures. If they do make any estimates, they should be careful to reveal all sources and to make sure that the buyer is informed that any such estimates should be verified independently.

case study

The case of *Furla v. Jon Douglas Co.* (1998) 65 C.A.4th 1069 involved a listing broker who had stated that a house was approximately 5,500 square feet but qualified it with "information deemed reliable but not guaranteed." The listing agent had received this information from the owner's daughter, who said it came from the architectural plans. During negotiations with the seller and the buyer's agent, Furla, the buyer, said, "OK! Fifty-five hundred square feet. I'll pay $170 a square foot." The offer was accepted.

When the buyer later decided to sell, an agent told him "a knowledgeable REALTOR® would easily recognize that the residence is substantially less than 5,500 square feet." Furla hired an appraiser who said it was 4,615 square feet. Another appraiser measured it at 4,437 square feet. Furla then sued the listing agent for negligent misrepresentation. While the superior court granted summary judgment for the listing broker, the court of appeal reversed, holding that there are genuine issues of material fact regarding whether the listing agent had the reasonable basis to report the house as 5,500 square feet and whether the buyer relied on this representation. The court of appeal emphasized that the square-feet estimate was not merely inaccurate, it was "grossly inaccurate" by more than 20 percent. The court remanded the issue to a jury.

Note: The selling broker was not sued, probably because the purchase contract strongly recommended that the buyer obtain independent inspections. It also stated that the buyer's agent made no representations as to the size of the structure.

■ Risk Area: Late Disclosures

Late disclosures can cause particular problems. While it is always better to disclose something, even if it is discovered late in the process, a known fact disclosed so late in the process that a buyer is put under duress can add an additional legal dimension to the situation.

case study

The case of *Jue v. Smiser* (1994) 23 C.A. 4th 312 involved a late disclosure. Buyers contracted to buy a home represented to have been designed by renowned architect Julia Morgan. The name Julia Morgan added to the prestige value of the property. However, three days before the close of escrow the sellers asked the buyers to sign a document acknowledging that there were no plans available that verified the architect. The buyers refused to sign but went through with the purchase. Then, discovering the house was not designed by Julia Morgan, the buyers sued the sellers and their broker for misrepresentation. The trial court held that there was no reliance on the misrepresentation because of the disclosure prior to the closing of escrow.

The court of appeal reversed the trial court, holding that it is not necessary that there be continuing reliance until the contract is executed.

Note: While full disclosure of detrimental facts learned is required prior to closing, the disclosure might not be enough to avoid liability. In a case such as this, the last-minute disclosure could place buyers in a position where they would have to complete the purchase or be homeless.

■ Recommendations

- Conduct the necessary visual inspection of the property in compliance with the *Easton* decision and document any possible defects you see. Even if you don't find any defects, make sure to document your visual inspection.

- Encourage sellers to be fully forthcoming on the Transfer Disclosure Statement.

- Practice how to explain to inquisitive buyers that the law only requires certain disclosures and not others.

- Create a checklist to make sure all property disclosures have occurred in each transaction.

- Never advertise square footage without disclosing the source of information and that it is unverified.

- Make sure all listing agreements recommend inspections by outside experts.

- Ensure that all disclosures are delivered promptly.

■ Unit 5 Review Quiz

1. Listing brokers should assist their sellers by filling out the owner's portion of the Transfer Disclosure Statement on behalf of the seller.

   a. True

   b. False

2. An agent would *MOST* likely have to inform a prospective purchaser about the

   a. triple murder in the home six months earlier.

   b. race of the previous occupants.

   c. former owner having died of AIDS five years ago.

   d. present owner having AIDS.

3. During the term of an escrow, a listing broker discovered that an addition to the building had been made without a building permit and that the addition was in violation of the building code. The broker should notify

   a. the buyer only.

   b. the seller only.

   c. both the buyer and the seller.

   d. neither, because the broker obtained this knowledge after the contract was entered into.

4. The *Easton* decision about required disclosures does *NOT* apply to

   a. single-family residences.

   b. defects that would be discovered by a reasonably competent inspection.

   c. nonresidential property.

   d. patent defects.

6

Risks Associated with Employment, Antitrust, Fair Housing, and Advertising

Risk Area: Employment Issues

California law places a special burden on the broker. While many sales associates are treated as independent contractors by the IRS, this status applies only to income tax withholding and Social Security contributions. It does not apply to broker liability.

Brokers will often use independent contractors in an attempt to avoid liability for acts of licensed associates or employees. Despite independent contractor agreements, real estate licensees are considered employees as to liability for torts (wrongful acts). The broker is liable for the torts of his or her employees within the scope of their employment. Likewise, independent contractor agreements do not appear to protect brokers from injury claims by salespersons under workers' compensation. Brokers, therefore, should obtain workers' compensation coverage.

Labor Code Section 2802(a) requires that an employer indemnify his or her employee for all necessary expenditures or losses incurred by the employee in direct consequence of the discharge of his or her duties or in obeying the lawful instructions of the employer. Because the sales associate is an employee of the broker for real estate purposes, the Labor Code provisions apply.

Risk Area: Broker Supervision

Section 10177(h) of the Business and Professions Code requires that brokers supervise their sales associates. Exercise of supervision precludes an independent contractor relationship. Therefore, a salesperson is an employee of his or her broker regardless of what the contract with the broker claims the relationship to be.

■ Risk Area: Antitrust Violations

The Sherman Antitrust Act of 1890 was enacted to prevent businesses from conspiring to control prices and/or competition. Penalties for violations include fines, damages, court costs, and up to three years' imprisonment. Antitrust violations include the following:

1. *Price-fixing*. It is illegal for a group of brokers to agree on minimum commissions that they would charge.
2. *Market allocation*. Agreements of firms to divide a marketplace geographically or by type of service are a violation because they reduce or eliminate competition.
3. *Group boycotting*. Firms may not agree to refuse to do business with a firm or individual. As an example, it is a violation of the act for two or more firms to agree not to allow another firm to show their listings.
4. *Tie-in agreements*. Agreements that require a business to buy additional goods or services in order to get the goods or services desired are illegal. An example of a tie-in agreement is the requirement that the buyer agree to keep the property insured through a firm controlled by the broker as a condition of submitting the buyer's offer.

The Cartwright Act is California's antitrust act that prohibits agreements restraining trade.

■ Risk Area: Fair Housing

Real estate licensees must comply with all federal and state fair housing laws. The laws include the following:

- *Civil Rights Act of 1866*. Citizens of all races shall have the same rights enjoyed by white citizens to inherit, purchase, lease, sell, or hold real and personal property.
- *Civil Rights Act of 1968 (Fair Housing Act)*. This act prohibits discrimination in housing based on race, color, sex, religion, or national origin. A 1988 amendment extended its coverage to the handicapped and children.
- *Unruh Civil Rights Act*. This act prohibits discrimination by a business on the basis of race, color, religion, ancestry, national origin, age, sex, and sexual preference.
- *Fair Employment and Housing Act (Rumford Act)*. This act prohibits discrimination based on race, color, religion, sex, marital status, national origin, or ancestry.
- *Business and Professions Code*. Provides for commissioner disciplinary action against licensees for discriminatory practices.

Because of overlapping coverage, a civil rights violation is likely to be a violation of several acts.

case study

Giebler v. M & B Associates a Limited Partnership (2003) 343 F.3d 1143 involved a plaintiff who has AIDS and is disabled. He had income of $837 per month from Social Security disability and between $300 and $400 per month from Housing Opportunities for People with AIDS.

Plaintiff was denied a rental because his income did not meet the landlord's requirements of three times the monthly rent, although his credit and rental history were good. The plaintiff's mother, who lived nearby and has adequate income and excellent credit, wanted to sign the lease but was rejected because of the landlord's policy of no cosigners.

Giebler brought action under the federal Fair Housing Amendment Act (FHAA), California's Fair Employment and Housing Act, and the Unruh Act alleging intentional discrimination for failure to reasonably accommodate Giebler's disability by refusal to accept a cosigner.

The U.S. District Court ruled for the landlord stating, "An accommodation which remedies the economic status of a disabled person is not an accommodation as contemplated by FHAA."

The 9th Circuit reversed, ruling that the FHAA includes reasonable economic accommodations to disabled tenant applicants rather than an inflexible rental policy barring cosigners. The court pointed out that renting to Giebler's mother would not be an economic burden to the landlord and would be a reasonable accommodation to a disabled resident.

Among the most common violations of fair housing laws is "steering," which is the channeling of prospective homebuyers to certain neighborhoods because of their racial or ethnic makeup.

■ Risk Area: Advertising

Agents may not use blind ads to attract buyers. A **blind ad** is one that fails to indicate that the advertiser is a licensed real estate professional and not a principal. Abbreviations like "bro." or "agt." are considered sufficient to designate a licensee.

A salesperson may not advertise any service without identifying the name of the employing broker.

False and misleading advertising is expressly prohibited. Licensees should exercise caution particularly in the distinction between puffing and misrepresentation. For example, advertising a property as a "Great Investment!" might well be effective in some cases. Used in an inappropriate instance, however, this could be problematic. If there were specific reasons why the property was *not* really a great investment, such a claim could possibly be viewed as misrepresentation if a purchaser lost money and sued.

Specific requirements are involved in advertising mobile homes, specifically that ads must be withdrawn within 48 hours of removal from the market.

The Truth-in-Lending Act (Regulation Z) regulates advertising related to lending. Certain trigger words create extended disclosure requirements.

Fair housing regulations prohibit the use of discriminatory advertising. More information can be found in Course 3 of this book.

The Federal Trade Commission regulates telemarketing and keeps the National Do Not Call Registry. The rules require cold callers to check the do-not-call registry. Even one offense of calling someone on the list can generate a complaint. Firms must also keep an internal list of those who have requested not to be contacted. Licensees should check both lists prior to making cold calls.

■ Recommendations

- ■ Practice how you present your brokerage fees/commissions to potential clients and customers. Never imply that a commission is "standard" or "customary."
- ■ If you find yourself dealing with a bigoted client, consider ending the relationship. At the very least, make sure the client knows you cannot and will not follow any instructions that violate fair housing laws.
- ■ Read all advertising carefully before it goes out. Research the HUD advisory bulletins to get guidance on which words to avoid in advertising property.

■ Unit 6 Review Quiz

1. Market allocation, price-fixing, and tie-in agreements are all violations of
   - a. antitrust laws.
   - b. fair housing laws.
   - c. advertising laws.
   - d. None of the above

2. The Civil Rights Act of 1968, as amended, does *NOT* prohibit
   - a. sex discrimination.
   - b. age discrimination.
   - c. discrimination against families.
   - d. discrimination against handicapped persons.

3. Which is an example of blind advertising?
   - a. Failure to advertise a location
   - b. Failure to indicate that the advertiser is an agent
   - c. Failure to include the name of the agent
   - d. Failure to include the price

4. In presenting two identical offers requiring seller financing to an owner, which act of the broker would be wrong?
   - a. Mentioning that one buyer had only recently been hired after a long period of unemployment
   - b. Mentioning that one buyer was black
   - c. Mentioning that one buyer had substantially greater income
   - d. Mentioning that one buyer had not given truthful credit information

5. A group of brokers in an area meet and agree that they will all charge a minimum commission of 5 percent. This is an example of
   - a. illegal price-fixing.
   - b. legal price-fixing.
   - c. illegal market allocation.
   - d. legal market allocation.

7 Legal Responsibility

This lesson covers what can happen if an action is taken against a licensee.

■ Discipline from the Department of Real Estate

The **Department of Real Estate,** which is also included in the Business, Transportation, and Housing Agency, is the primary state agency to administer California real estate law. The department was created by legislative act in 1917 and provided the first law in the United States for the licensing and regulation of real estate agents. These laws became a model for legislation in many other states.

Vicarious Liability

The broker can be held liable for the actions of his or her salespersons. The fact that a salesperson might be an independent contractor is irrelevant under California law. All salespersons are treated as employees under law.

Discipline Procedures

The real estate commissioner, appointed by the governor, is the chief executive officer of the department. The commissioner presides over meetings of the Real Estate Advisory Commission. The commissioner determines administrative policy and enforces the provisions of the real estate law in a manner that provides maximum protection for the purchasers of real property and those persons dealing with real estate licensees.

The **Administrative Procedure Act** authorizes the commissioner to hold formal hearings to determine issues involving a licensee, license applicant, or subdivider. After a hearing, the commissioner may suspend, revoke, or deny a license or halt sales in a subdivision.

The real estate commissioner does not have the authority to settle commission disputes. These matters are determined through a court of law; the state labor commissioner, the Department of Industrial Relations (for employer-employee disputes); or by arbitration if agreed to by the parties.

■ Criminal versus Civil Wrongs

Criminal wrongs involve crimes against the state for which the state provides penalties that include fines and/or imprisonment. Civil law involves wrongs committed against individuals for which damages are appropriate. A single act could involve both criminal and civil wrongs. As an example, an act of fraud, such as selling property that the seller does not own, could be criminal and subject the wrongdoer to criminal penalties and also entitle the victim to civil damages.

Most real estate cases are civil matters adjudicated between the parties, rather than criminal matters (where the defendant is charged by the state with a criminal offense).

■ Judicial Remedies

There are two types of judicial remedies available: monetary remedies and equitable remedies.

Monetary Remedies (Damages)

Compensatory damages are money damages to cover the loss for the injury sustained.

Exemplary (or punitive) **damages** go beyond actual compensation for an injury. They are awarded to punish the wrongdoer for an action that was aggravated by its willful nature, malice, fraud, or wanton and wicked conduct.

For example, if a seller forged a termite inspection report that indicated no infestation or damage and after the sale the purchaser discovered serious infestation and damage, a court might award the buyer actual costs to correct the problem (compensatory damages) plus exemplary or punitive damages to punish the seller for willful and outrageous conduct.

Nominal damages are monetary damages in a token sum such as $1. They are awarded to show a defendant was in the wrong but that no substantial damage to person, property, or reputation occurred. An example would be a trespass where a person crossed the land of another without permission or right but caused no damage.

Equitable Remedies

Remedies of conscience are the remedies available when judicial remedies are inadequate and equity or conscience demands them.

The court can force a person to perform as agreed. **Specific performance** is an equitable remedy usually awarded where money damages are inadequate.

Rescission is the mutual release of the parties to a contract. The contract is set aside, and the consideration that was given is returned. This equitable remedy would be used when promises were made because of a mutual mistake or when the contract became impossible to perform or the performance of the contract, while legal when the contract was made, became illegal because of a change in the law.

Through **reformation,** a court rewrites a contract to read as it was intended to be read by the parties rather than as stated. For example, a court would likely reform a lease that described the wrong premises when it was clear from the evidence which premises were intended to be leased.

Using an **injunction** as an equitable remedy, courts will order a party to cease and desist from an activity such as a trespass or a nuisance.

■ Alternative Dispute Resolution (ADR)

In addition to judicial remedies, nonjudicial remedies of arbitration and mediation are available to disputing parties.

Arbitration

Arbitration is a process for resolution of disputes. Many contracts call for mandatory arbitration, and the courts generally will enforce these agreements. The contracts usually provide for the choosing of the arbitrator and may state that the rules of the American Arbitration Association apply. In some cases, the courts can order nonbinding arbitration. Also, parties can agree to voluntary private arbitration in which the arbitrator serves much as a judge in hearing a case but is not bound by the legal rules of evidence or normal court formalities.

The principal benefits of arbitration are that it is faster and less expensive than court action. Matters that could take years before they are heard in court might be decided in days at a fraction of the cost that would have been incurred in a trial. Because of these benefits, arbitration has been gaining interest as a logical way to resolve disputes. However, parties agreeing to arbitrate disputes give up their legal rights to a jury trial, and the right to appeal the arbitrator's decision, even if it is contrary to established law. After the arbitrator makes a written decision, it can be presented to the local superior court for confirmation as a judgment of that court. At the court confirmation hearing, the judge cannot change the arbitrator's decision.

Professional real estate organizations often offer a medium for arbitration where issues such as commission disputes can be settled.

Mediation

Mediation is a process in which a neutral third party (mediator) works with the parties in a dispute to help them reach a satisfactory solution. The mediator suggests solutions and alternatives and might confer with the parties separately as well as together. Unlike an arbitrator, the mediator has no decision powers. The mediation process is not binding on the parties.

■ Self-Regulation of the Real Estate Industry

The National Association of REALTORS® has a process for enforcing its code of ethics. Complaints can be filed against members by other members or by buyers and sellers. The complaints go first to a grievance committee to determine whether the complaint is legitimate, and then to a professional standards hearing.

■ Unit 7 Review Quiz

1. Damages awarded by a court in excess of actual damages suffered by a plaintiff are known as
   a. liquidated damages.
   b. nominal damages.
   c. exemplary damages.
   d. compensatory damages.

2. *MOST* lawsuits involving real estate matters can be described as
   a. criminal proceedings.
   b. administrative agency actions.
   c. common-law actions.
   d. civil actions.

3. The remedy in which a person is ordered to cease and desist from an activity is known as
   a. reformation.
   b. specific performance.
   c. an injunction.
   d. None of the above

4. The process whereby a third person works to resolve a problem but cannot impose a decision on the parties is known as
   a. arbitration.
   b. mediation.
   c. specific performance.
   d. quiet title.

■ Risk Reduction

The risks associated with the real estate industry are vast and can seem overwhelming. No single course or training program can discuss or prevent all risks.

Risk reduction is based on following some simple guidelines: planning, training, implementing and enforcing office policies, and ongoing education are essential elements in reducing risk and creating a risk management culture.

A risk management culture is not one where everyone is constantly terrified of being sued. It is one where proactive steps are taken to anticipate, reduce, and control risks.

Risks arise primarily from sloppy execution of key tasks, from a lack of knowledge, from a lack of proper supervision, or from failure to follow established policies and procedures.

All brokerages, no matter their size, should foster frequent training programs and discussions on managing risk. Since avoiding risk usually means regularly performing the tasks required of licensees, this is also good business.

It is highly recommended that brokerage companies adopt an official risk management policy documenting expected practices and procedures. The practical everyday elements of managing risk, and all policies associated with risk, should be discussed regularly with licensees. Consequences of illegal or unethical behavior should be outlined in brokerage meetings, not to instill fear, but to place proper focus and priority on risk management.

Licensees should be encouraged to come to their supervising brokers with questions. And, above all, licensees should be encouraged—in fact, required—to inform their supervising broker whenever they have the slightest concern that a client or customer is unhappy with a transaction and may have any type of legal claim. Above all, licensees should stay current on new laws and on court cases that clarify or change what is expected of them.

■ A Last Word on Risk Management

This course has reviewed key laws and regulations and provided specific real-life case examples for you to consider.

However, it is worth noting that perhaps the best way to avoid litigation is to treat those with whom and for whom you work not just legally and ethically, but also with understanding, compassion, and courtesy.

In his best-selling book *Blink,* Malcolm Gladwell discusses a research study that attempted to predict the likelihood a doctor would be sued by a patient simply by analyzing a small bit of interaction between the doctor and a patient.

The study couldn't tell the quality of the doctor's diagnostic ability, but still was able to predict to a remarkable degree which doctors would be the subjects of lawsuits and which ones wouldn't. Why? Because whether the patient believed the doctor cared and was genuinely doing their best and paying true attention to the patient's needs played an enormous role in whether a patient would sue that doctor if he or she made a mistake.

Doctors who showed concern and compassion and who listened carefully to patients were far less likely to be sued than those who did not.

The point is simple. A large part of risk management is learning about and following the law and acting ethically, and this course has focused on those aspects. But another key component is simply treating clients and customers with due consideration.

No course can make you care, but caring can keep you from getting sued.

Unit 1 Review Answers

1. **a.** E&O insurance is intended to protect the broker from the costs associated with lawsuits.
2. **b.** Because E&O insurance is intended to protect against the most expensive liabilities, brokers should consider lowering the costs of the insurance by increasing the deductible rather than lowering coverage.
3. **b.** Licensees should avoid providing negligent advice and refer buyers and sellers to experts in the field.
4. **d.** E&O insurance protects against lawsuits.
5. **c.** A calm and considerate response to complaints can go a long way toward satisfying a party otherwise inclined to sue. Gather all relevant information before making a response and seek legal guidance.

Unit 2 Review Answers

1. **c.** The statement is general enough that it would likely be considered a clear statement of opinion.
2. **a.** Fraud is intentional deceit to induce a party to act to his or her detriment.
3. **a.** The case of *Ford v. Cournale* (1974) 36 C.A.3d 172 held that providing income data based on 100 percent occupancy was misrepresentation for which the broker could be held liable.
4. **a.** While the case law is not definitive, some courts have held licensees to a higher standard of care when dealing with inexperienced buyers.

Unit 3 Review Answers

1. **b.** Net listings are legal but discouraged in California. The broker must disclose how much commission will be received.
2. **a.** An option listing does not require the broker to purchase the property if a buyer is not found; it simply gives the broker the option to purchase. All the other answer choices list requirements involved with an option listing.
3. **c.** Because this would probably be considered a secret profit, a court would likely find that no commission is due.
4. **d.** Compensation does not determine agency, so an agency can receive compensation only from one party but represent both as an agent. Dual agents must protect confidential information for both parties.

Unit 4 Review Answers

1. **c.** All offers must be disclosed until the transaction has closed.
2. **a.** The fact that the owner will accept less than the listed price is confidential information that the listing agent must protect. The other answer choices reflect material facts that the licensee would be obligated to disclose.
3. **c.** Such a request should be discussed with the seller principal before any response is provided. The seller could determine whether that information should be revealed and to whom.
4. **c.** Salespersons must deliver trust fund checks to their broker. The broker, depending on the circumstances, may hold the check until the offer is accepted.

Unit 5 Review Answers

1. **b.** Sellers should fill out the owner's portion of the Transfer Disclosure Statement.
2. **a.** A recent triple murder could well be deemed a material fact, and thus it is advisable for such an occurrence to be disclosed. The other choices all are clearly items that should NOT be disclosed.
3. **c.** This would be considered a material fact that would need to be disclosed to both the client (the seller) and to customers (potential buyers).
4. **c.** In the case of *Smith v. Rickard* (1989) 205 C.A.3d 1354, the court indicated that the affirmative duty to conduct a reasonable inspection does not extend to nonresidential or agricultural property.

Unit 6 Review Answers

1. **a.** Market allocation, price-fixing, and tie-in agreements are violations of antitrust laws.
2. **b.** Age discrimination is not prohibited by federal fair housing laws.
3. **b.** A blind ad is one that fails to indicate that the advertiser is an agent and not a principal.
4. **b.** Mentioning the race of the offeror would make the agent and seller liable for charges of discrimination.
5. **a.** Commission rates are negotiable, and attempts by brokers to establish "standard" or "minimum" commissions would be illegal price-fixing under antitrust laws.

Unit 7 Review Answers

1. **c.** Exemplary (or punitive) damages go beyond actual compensation for an injury. They are awarded to punish the wrongdoer for an action that was aggravated by its willful nature, malice, fraud, or wanton and wicked conduct.
2. **d.** Most lawsuits stemming from real estate transactions are civil rather than criminal in nature.
3. **c.** With an injunction, courts order a party to cease and desist from an activity such as a trespass or a nuisance.
4. **b.** Unlike an arbitrator, the mediator has no decision powers. The mediation process is not binding on the parties.